LIPPINCOTT'S CLASSICS
EDITED BY EDWIN L. MILLER, A.M.
PRINCIPAL OF THE NORTHWESTERN HIGH SCHOOL, DETROIT, MICH.

COLERIDGE'S
THE RIME OF THE ANCIENT MARINER
AND OTHER POEMS

WITH INTRODUCTION, NOTES AND AN APPENDIX
BY
LOUISE POUND, Ph.D.
PROFESSOR OF THE ENGLISH LANGUAGE, UNIVERSITY OF NEBRASKA

PHILADELPHIA AND LONDON
J. B. LIPPINCOTT COMPANY

COPYRIGHT, 1920, BY J. B. LIPPINCOTT COMPANY
ALL RIGHTS RESERVED

PRINTED BY J. B. LIPPINCOTT COMPANY
AT THE WASHINGTON SQUARE PRESS
PHILADELPHIA, U. S. A.

This scarce antiquarian book is included in our special *Legacy Reprint Series*. In the interest of creating a more extensive selection of rare historical book reprints, we have chosen to reproduce this title even though it may possibly have occasional imperfections such as missing and blurred pages, missing text, poor pictures, markings, dark backgrounds and other reproduction issues beyond our control. Because this work is culturally important, we have made it available as a part of our commitment to protecting, preserving and promoting the world's literature. Thank you for your understanding.

LIPPINCOTT'S CLASSICS—VOL. IV
EDITED BY EDWIN L. MILLER, A.M.
PRINCIPAL OF THE NORTHWESTERN HIGH SCHOOL, DETROIT, MICH.

SAMUEL TAYLOR COLERIDGE
THE ANCIENT MARINER, AND OTHER POEMS

LIPPINCOTT'S CLASSICS
EDITED BY EDWIN L. MILLER, A.M.
PRINCIPAL OF THE NORTHWESTERN HIGH SCHOOL, DETROIT, MICH.

BURKE'S CONCILIATION
With Notes By E. L. MILLER, A.M.

SHAKESPEARE'S MACBETH
With Notes By CHAS. R. GASTON

SHAKESPEARE'S MIDSUMMER NIGHT'S DREAM
With Notes By CLARENCE STRATTON

COLERIDGE'S THE RIME OF THE ANCIENT MARINER AND OTHER POEMS
With Notes By LOUISE POUND, PH.D.

TENNYSON'S IDYLLS OF THE KING
With Notes By WILLIS H. WILCOX, PH.M.

SCOTT'S LADY OF THE LAKE
With Notes By J. MILNOR DOREY, A.M.

AMERICAN ORATORS
With Notes By CLARENCE STRATTON

IN PREPARATION

SHAKESPEARE'S JULIUS CÆSAR
With Notes By MISS MARY McKITTRICK

DICKENS'S TALE OF TWO CITIES
With Notes By W. WILBUR HATFIELD

SCOTT'S IVANHOE
With Notes By T. H. BAIR

SHAKESPEARE'S TEMPEST
With Notes By O. J. P. WIDSTOE

GEORGE ELIOT'S SILAS MARNER
With Notes By WILLIAM M. OTTO

LINCOLN'S SPEECHES
With Notes By J. de ROULHAC HAMILTON

BURNS'S POEMS
With Notes By E. L. MILLER

BOSWELL'S JOHNSON
With Notes By J. M. SKINNING

PREFATORY NOTE

In addition to *The Ancient Mariner*, there have been included in this edition, as adding to its convenience for school usage, several other poems often read by young students, notably *Christabel* and *Kubla Khan*. Coleridge's political odes and his personal poems deserve a place in the study of his poetry, but they are more attractive to mature than to younger readers and are not very often read by the latter.

Coleridge's poems, *The Ancient Mariner* especially, have been edited many times. The chief features in which the present edition may claim departure from its predecessors are, first, the inclusion in the Appendix of a variety of illustrative passages, bearing on the poems, which should prove valuable in a school edition, and should save time for teacher and pupil; and, second, the inclusion in the notes on *The Ancient Mariner* of an unusual number of earlier readings of amended passages. These may be passed over by the student who prefers to have before him only the poem in its final form; but they are often instructive, as well as interesting, if inquiry for the reasons for the changes be made.

The texts of the poems reproduce those of Ernest Hartley Coleridge's edition of Coleridge's poetry, issued in 1912, which is based on the last edition of the poems published in the author's lifetime, namely, the three-volume Pickering edition of 1834. *The Ancient Mariner*, in the form in which it originally appeared, may be found in Thomas Hutchinson's reprint of the *Lyrical Ballads*, London, 1907.

LOUISE POUND.

LINCOLN, NEBR., 1920.

CONTENTS

	PAGE
Introduction to The Ancient Mariner	9
The Ancient Mariner	33
Introduction to Christabel and Kubla Khan	61
Christabel	70
Kubla Khan	90
Fancy in Nubibus	92
Time Real and Imaginary	93
The Devil's Thoughts	94
France	95
Love	99
Answer to a Child's Question	103
Youth and Age	104
Lesson for a Boy	106
The Homeric Hexameter	106
Hexameter and Pentameter	106
Letter to William and Dorothy Wordsworth	107
The Knight's Tomb	109
Epitaph	110
Notes	111
Questions	132
Appendix	136

INTRODUCTION TO THE ANCIENT MARINER

THE TIMES

Political and Literary Conditions.—The period extending through the reigns of George III and George IV, marked on the continent by the French Revolution and the Napoleonic Wars, has strong interest not only for English but for general European literature. The transition from the eighteenth to the nineteenth century brought profound changes in literary ideals, as well as in political thinking. The poetry of the preceding era, having for its great names Dryden and Pope and their followers, had placed chief emphasis upon formal elegance and correctness. They had expressed themselves mainly in the poetic form known as the heroic couplet, which they handled, not with the freedom of Chaucer and the Elizabethans, but in a certain set way. In the treatment of their subject-matter, they prized "wit," lucidity, and reasonableness, and disliked enthusiasm, the emotional, or the bizarre. Forerunners of the change, which came in full tide at about the border of the centuries, were Collins, Gray, Goldsmith, Cowper, Crabbe, and especially Burns. The movement is known usually as the "Romantic" movement. It was, in general, one of liberation, of emancipation from limitations, whether in form or in subject-matter. Men cared again for spontaneity and for unchecked expression of the emotions. They looked inward, giving free rein to the expression of the individual, or they looked outward toward the remote, the unusual, the marvellous. They developed new democratic and humanitarian ideals; the more radical wished to level existing social distinctions. They felt an ardor for wild nature, and recognized a deep sympathy between man and nature, not before known

Introduction to the Ancient Mariner

in English or in European poetry. Again, as in the sixteenth century, there was a widened horizon and a consequent flood-tide of poetic energy. The *Lyrical Ballads* of Wordsworth and Coleridge, published in 1798, and having as its first poem *The Ancient Mariner,* is often looked upon as a poetic landmark, registering the conscious arrival of this literary revolution.

SAMUEL TAYLOR COLERIDGE

Parentage and Early Education.—Coleridge was born October 21, 1772, at Ottery St. Mary's in Devonshire, the youngest child, by a second marriage, of a large family. His father was vicar of the village and schoolmaster, an auspicious parentage for a boy early devoted to books and early showing a vivid imagination. In reminiscences of this period written in later life, he tells of his acting out his boyish reading among the docks and thistles and nettles of the churchyard; for instance, of his slashing with a stick at rows of nettles representing the "Seven Champions of Christendom." His father died when Coleridge was about nine years old, and through the efforts of friends he was admitted to Christ's Hospital, the famous charity school at London. Here also went Charles Lamb, later the author of *Essays of Elia,* who became Coleridge's youthful associate and lifelong friend. They were well taught as "blue-coat" boys, of whom there were seven hundred, garbed in long belted coats and yellow stockings. Coleridge was among the best scholars, and left a good record. Like many precocious children, he was rather solitary. Testimony is to the effect that he liked to read and dream, and felt indisposition to boyish sports. A characteristic anecdote tells that one day, when Coleridge was walking the streets and swinging his arms in a strange manner, he chanced to touch the pocket of an old gentleman who was passing. The latter was about to hand him over to the police as a pickpocket. "I am not a pickpocket," the boy protested. "I only thought I was Leander swimming the Hellespont." This answer prompted the old gentleman to subscribe to a circulating library in order to give Leander all the reading he wished, and he read through the library, the story continues, without skipping a volume. Lamb speaks of the "deep, sweet intonations" with which Coleridge recited

Samuel Taylor Coleridge

Greek hexameters in his youthful days at Christ's Hospital, and expounded abstruse philosophers like Jamblichus and Plotinus, to casual passers, until " the walls of the old Grey Friars re-echoed to the accents of the inspired charity boy." Lamb's essay, *Christ's Hospital Five-and-Thirty Years Ago*,[1] describes the school as seen through his eyes; the whole essay may well be read by the student. Prophetic of Coleridge's lifelong impulsiveness and lack of balanced judgment was his attempt to escape the school, when fifteen, by apprenticing himself to a cobbler. In his days at Christ's Hospital Coleridge began to be what he always was—a good talker. In this period, too, he felt the first strong poetic enthusiasm of his life, that for the sonnets of the minor poet, William Lisle Bowles.

Life at Cambridge and Marriage.—Coleridge entered Cambridge in the fall of 1791, having won a scholarship at Jesus College. He read much and talked much, but proved to be an unsteady student. He was serious at first, but irregular later. Like Wordsworth and Southey, with whom he was afterwards to be associated, he assimilated, in his undergraduate days, the generous radical enthusiasms of the French Revolutionary era, views which all three—Coleridge first—were afterwards to discard for greater conservatism. Coleridge was absent from Cambridge during the winter months of 1793–94. Actuated by some sudden impulse, or because of difficulties of some kind, he enlisted in the Fifteenth Light Dragoons, under the name of Silas Tomkyns Comberback. He made a poor dragoon. The influence on his character might perhaps have been salutary, had he remained in service long enough to feel the effect of military regularity and discipline, qualities he was sadly to need. As it turned out, his acquaintance with Latin soon caught the attention of his superior officer, who procured Coleridge's release in April, and he was reinstated at Cambridge. Here he remained some time longer, although he never took his degree.

---
[1] *Appendix, p. 129.*

Samuel Taylor Coleridge

In June of that year, in a visit at Oxford, he was introduced to Southey, who was later to be poet laureate. In August of the same year, he went to Bristol with Southey, making the acquaintance there of several other young persons, having like himself radical social ideals. They planned the establishment of an ideal social community, to be called a "Pantisocracy," or "government by all," in the New World. The name was Coleridge's. "Twelve gentlemen of good education and liberal principles were to embark with twelve ladies" . . . for some "delightful part of the new back settlement of America." They were to work at the soil and to enjoy freedom of thought and action. They chose for its site the banks of the Susquehanna, which they liked for its soft-flowing name. Among the Pantisocrats was Robert Lovell, who had married Mary Fricker, to whose sister, Edith, Southey was engaged. Each of the emigrants to the Susquehanna was to take with him a wife, and the third Fricker sister, Sarah, being sympathetic with the project and free, seemed designated by Fate for Coleridge. On the impulse of the moment, apparently, he proceeded to fall in love with her, engaged himself to her, although without prospects or resources, and in 1795, just before the marriage of her sister to Southey, they were married. The Pantisocracy scheme could not be carried out, for lack of funds, and finally came to nothing.

Coleridge's Great Poetic Period.—Coleridge at this time had no money and no fixed occupation. The sole prospective income on which he married was an order from a Bristol publisher named Cottle for a book of poems, for which a small sum was to be paid. These were published in 1796, when Coleridge was twenty-four. In comparison with his later work the quality of these juvenile poems was not notable. He also attempted preaching,[2] lecturing, and journalism, establishing a short-lived periodical called *The Watchman*. Meantime, the family was living at Bristol and at the neighboring village of Clevedon, helped by the presence

[2] Appendix, p. 129.

Samuel Taylor Coleridge

of a boarder. It was at Clevedon that his family was increased by the birth of his son Hartley, the first of his three children. This was relatively a happy period for Coleridge, but ominous, too; for it was in 1795 that he began taking drugs, for neuralgic or rheumatic pains, a practice which was to take firm hold of him and to shadow his whole succeeding life.

In 1797, at the suggestion of a friend to whom he was indebted for generous assistance, Coleridge—having yet no permanent occupation—removed with his family to a tiny cottage in the village of Nether Stowey in Somersetshire. Here he was visited by Lamb and by Wordsworth, whose acquaintance he had made not long before. Soon the Coleridges were joined by Wordsworth and his sister Dorothy, who took a cottage in the neighboring village of Alfoxden, about three miles away.[3] They saw each other daily and became lifelong friends. The association was to mean everything to Coleridge; indeed it was the great event of his life. Coleridge's companionship had influence on Wordsworth; but on Coleridge Wordsworth's strong mind and character, and the quick comprehension and sympathy of his gifted sister, were immediately stimulating. Under favorable conditions, had she been educated like her brother, and encouraged to production, Dorothy might herself have become a great writer like her companions. All the best work of both poets was done under her influence. The effect of the society of the Wordsworths upon Coleridge was magical. His genius suddenly ripened into imaginative power and dreamy musical expression; and within the year he produced nearly all his best work. He was yet in excellent health, though excitable and restless, and he was at the height of his imaginative powers. Wordsworth and he undertook the *Lyrical Ballads* in partnership[4]; but Wordsworth proved to be so much more productive that by the time the volume was ready for publication Wordsworth had nine-

---
[3] Appendix, p. 131.
[4] *Appendix, p. 135.*

Samuel Taylor Coleridge

teen pieces ready for it, and Coleridge but four, chief among which was *The Ancient Mariner*. From these, his most productive days, come, beside his pieces in the *Lyrical Ballads*, the First Part of *Christabel; Frost at Midnight; France: an Ode; Lewti: or the Circassian Love-Chaunt; The Nightingale; The Dark Ladie;* and *Kubla Khan*. Possibly something of the great power of his poetry of this period is due to the heightening effect on his imagination of opium-taking. Under the stress of physical and mental suffering, to help him throw off depression, or to arouse his powers—though he concealed the fact for a time from his friends—he became more and more enslaved by the drug, until by 1803 he was its confirmed victim. If it helped him in the beginning, it was soon of great harm to him, and undoubtedly was a chief contributing cause of his failure as a man and of his loss of power as a poet. Within the next two years came two poems which complete the list of his best works. The Second Part of *Christabel* was composed in 1802, and in 1804 came *Dejection*, a tragic utterance, recognized as one of the greatest personal odes in the language, in which he laments the passing from him of his gift of poetic creation.

The Next Years.—The rest of Coleridge's life was a record of disappointments and failures, leaving one with a sense of the waste of unequalled powers. The same standards did not hold then as now with regard to the acceptance by literary men of benevolences from patrons or friends; but, for Coleridge, his dependence upon others began early and lasted throughout his life. From the first, he was incapable of the support of himself or his family; but he had the gift of personal charm, and never lost the power to fascinate new friends who were willing to assist him. As early as 1797 he accepted an annuity from the Wedgwoods, famous manufacturers of pottery, in order that he might be free to devote himself to great things. This annuity was paid to Coleridge or to his family until 1814, when it was withdrawn—justly enough, since it had failed of its purpose, the stimulating of productivity on Coleridge's part. After

Samuel Taylor Coleridge

the period at Nether Stowey, his life was a wandering one, mostly a forlorn record of projects deferred, or estrangements from friends and from his wife—with whom a kind of separation was arranged in 1810—of broken promises, and of disordered ways. Advantages were not wanting to him, but they resulted in little. In 1798 he went abroad with the Wordsworths to Germany, his expenses being borne by the Wedgwoods. He learned German, and he matriculated at the University of Göttingen, where he worked hard at metaphysics, and acquired his taste for German transcendental philosophy, which he brought back and tried to interpret for England. He was again in England in 1799, living chiefly in London and in the Lake region with his brother-in-law, Southey—upon whom fell mostly the care of Coleridge's family. In 1804, on funds supplied by Wordsworth, he went to Malta and Italy. Returning, penniless and unemployed, he lived at various places, helped by various friends, and continued miscellaneous activities, as journalist, lecturer, magazine editor, dramatist, and translator. De Quincey at one time gave him £300; he had assistance also from Lord Byron and others; and in 1814 he was given a small pension by the King. He was always a trial to his friends and was often estranged from them, even for short intervals with Wordsworth; but in the end he retained all his friendships while never losing the power to make others. He had the ways, the look, the face of a genius, and he had the power of mind. Wordsworth thought him " the most wonderful man that ever lived," and so did others.

During 1813 and 1814 he was almost hopelessly and entirely under opium influence. The chronicle of these years is a chronicle of half-attempts, of failures, and of promises which did not materialize in achievement. He lacked in self-control. His conscience remained keen, and his sense of religious faith was strong, but he found himself unable to respond to the demands of duty. It would be difficult to find a more pathetic example of weak will, vacillating purpose, physical irresolution, and hampering indolence.

Samuel Taylor Coleridge

Later Life.—The last years of Coleridge's life were accompanied by a partial regeneration, and were happier. He managed partly to free himself from subjection to opium. In April, 1816, he placed himself under the surveillance of Dr. James Gillman of Highgate, who received him into his house, and helped him gradually to restrict his use of drugs. He improved in spirits, and achieved comparatively even health. Hither came many celebrities, among them Emerson and Carlyle,[5] to visit him. Our last picture of him is as the "Sage of Highgate," a sort of oracle, surrounded by eager disciples, in a rôle much like that of Ben Jonson at the Mermaid Tavern, or of Dr. Johnson in the London taverns. He was one of the most wonderful talkers of whom there is record, and to hear his conversation was the magnet which all his life drew so many to him.[6] By it he exercised, says Carlyle, wide influence during these last days. His death came in 1834, when he was sixty-two.

Coleridge's Work.—A view of Coleridge's writings reveals the dispersive rather than the concentrated character of his mind and work. His verse is largely a collection of fragments, and most of his prose work is unfinished. Considering the high place it has won, his poetry does not bulk very large; it is better known from anthologies than from collected editions. Yet, for its quantity, it exhibits unwonted variety. The group making strongest popular impression consists of his mystical, supernatural, or romantic poems, *The Ancient Mariner, Christabel*, or the fragment *Kubla Khan*—a vein which he soon worked out. The political pieces, *Ode to a Departing Year*, and *France: an Ode*, represent another vein which he soon exhausted. Some of his strongest and most distinctive work belongs to yet a third group, consisting of meditative, or confessional, or autobiographic pieces, such as *Frost at Midnight, Dejection, To Wordsworth*. The small group of his love poems is relatively negligible. His dramas include *The Fall of Robe-*

---
[5] Appendix, p. 131.
[6] Appendix, p. 133.

Samuel Taylor Coleridge

spierre, an early effort written in collaboration with Southey; *Wallenstein*, translated from the German of Schiller; *Remorse*, earlier named *Osorio*, acted in 1813 through the intervention of Lord Byron; and *Zapolya*, published in 1817. His prose is of miscellaneous character, and is hardly of the volume or the quality commensurate with his gifts as a scholar and a critic and his genius as a writer. He published a *Life of Robespierre* in 1784, and a prose phantasy, *The Wanderings of Cain*, in 1798; in journalism he contributed to *The Watchman*, 1796; to *The Friend*, 1809-10, and articles to *The Morning Post, The Courier*, etc. Two of his *Lay Sermons* were published in 1816 and 1817. Of greatest significance are his critical writings, found in his *Biographia Literaria*, 1817, and in his Shakespeare Lectures, and scattered essays and notes upon philosophical subjects. A volume of *Table Talk*, edited by his nephew, Henry Nelson Coleridge, was published after his death.

Coleridge as a Poet.—Several qualities give special effect to Coleridge's poetry, and have won for it distinctive place. One is his literally *visionary* power, his ability to imagine scenes as vivid as those in dreams, and to clothe them in words. Coleridge was always much concerned with the psychology of dreams, apparitions, and mental illusions of all kinds. Another distinctive quality is his gift of musicianship with words. At its best, Coleridge's verse is unconscious, spontaneous, and it charms by its liquid flow, and mystic, elfin melody. In *Kubla Khan*, his gift of mellifluous flow, his power to dream vivid scenes, and to create a mystical romantic " atmosphere," have made the poem unforgettable, although it makes no appeal to the mind; it is but a fragment, devoid of the logical sequence of ideas. Coleridge was the real beginner, for English poetry, of literary ballads of the weird supernatural. He was also the inaugurator of poetry of self-conscious analysis, or of autobiographic confession, like *Frost at Midnight*, or *Dejection*. Prose writers, like Bunyan and Jonathan Edwards, and religious poets, like Cowper, had looked into their own

Samuel Taylor Coleridge

souls and re-lived their inward life before the world, urged by their consciences and fearful lest they fail of true religious devotion; but, in English secular poetry, we find poetry of this kind first with Wordsworth and Coleridge. Wordsworth portrays, with a sense of responsibility, the growth, or the processes, of his own mind. He sets forth his inward life for the good of the world, hoping to teach others. Coleridge is more confessional than didactic; he gives us poetry of temperament. He depicts the subtle shades of his own emotion, his fevered moods, his feelings of lassitude, languor, or collapse. All that he sees is colored by self-thought, and he projects his abnormal mental moods on outward nature. Poems like *Dejection* and *To Wordsworth* illustrate the third vein of poetry which he tried and worked out. Neither of the three leading types which he attempted was a type likely to be inexhaustible, and it was perhaps owing to this, as well as to his collapse as a man, that he ceased so early to be poetically creative.

THE ANCIENT MARINER

Composition and Textual History.—The origin of the poem as a "pot boiler," planned to defray the expenses of a walking tour, in the days when verse commanded greater money returns than prose, has been told by Coleridge himself, and may best be read in his words.[1] Wordsworth had been reading Shelvocke's *Voyages*,[2] and suggested that the hero be a seaman who had been accursed for the crime of killing an albatross. This was to be taken for the groundwork. As the poem became too long for the magazine poem they had planned, they thought of composing a volume of poems in two distinct styles, one to be exemplified by Coleridge, the other by Wordsworth.[3] *The Ancient Mariner* appeared anonymously as the initial poem in *Lyrical Ballads*, 1798. It was longer than in its present form, and was thickly sprinkled with archaic spellings and with old words from Chaucer and Spenser and the ballads. Wordsworth thought the poem was one reason for the failure of the *Lyrical Ballads*, and Coleridge wished to omit it from the second edition. It was reprinted, however, with a few textual changes, in 1800, and with this note by Wordsworth:

> The author was himself very desirous that it should be suppressed. This has arisen from a consciousness of the defects of the poem; and from a knowledge that many persons had been displeased with it. The poem of my friend has, indeed, many great defects; first, that the principal person has no distinct character, either in his profession of Mariner, or as a human being who, having been long under the control of supernatural impressions, might be supposed himself to partake of

---

[1] Appendix, p. 134.
[2] Appendix, p. 134.
[3] Appendix, p. 135.

The Ancient Mariner

something supernatural; secondly, that he does not act but is constantly acted upon; thirdly, that the events having no necessary connection, do not produce each other; and, lastly, that the imagery is somewhat too laboriously accumulated. Yet the poem contains many delicate touches of passion, and, indeed, the passion is everywhere true to nature; a great many of the stanzas present beautiful images, and are expressed with unusual felicity of language; and the versification, though the meter is in itself unfit for long poems, is harmonious and artfully varied, exhibiting the utmost power of that meter, and every variety of which it is capable. It, therefore, appeared to me that these several merits (the first of which, namely, that of the passion, is of the highest kind) gave to the poem a value which is not often possessed by better poems. On this account, I requested of my friend to permit me to republish it.

The poem was first printed, in its present form, in the *Sibylline Leaves*, a collection of Coleridge's poems made in 1817. The marginal glosses, or quaint prose commentary on the narrative, and the motto from Burnet were added in this edition, certain lines were slightly changed, and many archaisms of spelling and vocabulary were discarded.

Materials of the Poem.—In both manner and form, the chief indebtedness of *The Ancient Mariner* is to the romantic and legendary ballads of England and Scotland, in the atmosphere of which Coleridge was thoroughly steeped. Among them are many ballads of the weird supernatural—his debt to which is general rather than particular; and there are sea-ballads, one of which, "The grand old ballad of Sir Patrick Spens," he mentions at the opening of his autobiographical ode *Dejection*. The ballad influence, aside from stanzaic form and language, is seen chiefly in stray touches in the handling, in the apparent artlessness and simplicity of the narrative, and in the conveyance of shudder. Words-worth and Coleridge had also been reading German ballads,

The Ancient Mariner

among them Bürger's *Lenore,* one of the most striking ballads of the weird supernatural in literature.

Other elements entering into the poem are saints' legends, accounts of South Sea voyages, and a dream of Coleridge's friend, Mr. Cruikshank, of a skeleton ship.[4] A possible source may have been Captain Thomas James's *Strange and Dangerous Voyage . . . in His Intended Discovery of the North-West Passage into the South Sea,* London, 1633.[5] Coleridge may also have known a letter written by Paulinus, Bishop of Nola, in the fourth century—telling of an old man who is the sole survivor of the crews of a shipwrecked fleet, and of the navigation of his ship by a " crew of angels," steered by the " Pilot of the World." In the wedding scene, a hint may have been taken, one critic thinks, from the poem *Alonzo the Brave and the Fair Imogene* by Coleridge's contemporary, Matthew Lewis. But whether, or how far, Coleridge was indebted to these sources is mainly of speculative interest. What he did to his groundwork, rather than where he found it, is of interest to the student of his poetry. His main wish was to find materials, or to follow models, free from present-day associations.

The Ancient Mariner does not subject itself readily to localization in time and space. Attempts to fix its chronology or its geography are as unprofitable as for Spenser's *Faerie Queene,* or for the first part of *Christabel.* Voyages to the tropical seas of the Pacific and polar explorations are modern, and so is the sentiment of animal sanctity modern. Neither the geography of the poem nor the leading sentiment it expresses were within the horizon of the Middle Ages. A few touches are specific. The region from which the Mariner embarks and to which he returns, his " own countree," with its " kirk," is obviously the " North Countrie " of the ballads. But the North Countrie did not send out ships to the Pacific or to the Arctic seas. For the rest, the suggestions are as mediæval as those in *Christabel;*

---

[4] Appendix, p. 134.
[5] See note on l. 61, p. 112.

The Ancient Mariner

for instance, the hermit who shrieves, the vesper bell, the ejaculation " gramercy," the reference to " Mary Mother," and the exclamations:

> By Him who died on cross:
>
> Heaven's Mother send us grace:
>
>   O Christ,
> That ever this should be!

Mediæval also is the Catholic idea of penance and expiation. On the secular side, the crossbow is a mediæval " property," and the bride's garden " bower," and the " merry minstrelsy " are mediæval. The spelling in the first edition was old, and so are many of the words; and the glosses are in the mediæval manner. The symbolic way in which the albatross is used is almost the only way in which animal life appears in older literature. It is hardly a real bird at all, but stands for something in the moral world.

Distinctive when the poem was published was the sea element in it. The sea played a large part in English poetry before the Norman Conquest; then it all but vanished for centuries. It reappeared in poetry of the nineteenth century, beginning mainly with *The Ancient Mariner*, and this element was a large factor in the success of the poem. A majority of the purchasers of the first edition are said to have been sea-faring men. It is the real sea, too, which appears in Coleridge's poem, with its changing moods, its fresh breeze alternating with calm, its dazzling ice-fields, copper sky, and phosphorescent lights; but it has also all the wildness and wonder of a dream sea. The setting of dread events which Coleridge obtains by isolating his characters in a dim wood or in a feudal castle at midnight in *Christabel*, he obtains by isolating them on a wide, wide sea in *The Ancient Mariner*. He promptly removes his story to a region where marvels are plausible.

Structure.—*The Ancient Mariner* has for its encompassing action the wedding feast, with its guests, music, and

The Ancient Mariner

progress, which sets the narrative in motion, and helps to bring it to a close. It affords the only normal human element in the poem, and serves to connect the marvellous tale of the Mariner, set in mid-ocean, with the actual life that we know. The reversions to its progress which interrupt now and then the Mariner's story, help to break the monotony and to heighten the contrasts. As for the narrative itself, the striking thing, as Coleridge handles it, is the rapidity of its events and the terseness and convincingness with which they are told. These qualities are unique for Coleridge in this poem. He is more likely, elsewhere in his verse, to be too profuse or turgid, not to know where to stop, than he is to show such retrenchment or restraint as in *The Ancient Mariner*. The brevity of the introduction has often been pointed out. Hardly fifty lines, and the boat is out on mid-ocean, its characters before us, the narrative fully launched. Details are few but clear, and events follow in such breathless succession that the reader has no time to doubt. Pivotal happenings are the shooting of the albatross, the apparition of the dice-playing figures on the spectre ship, the death of the Mariner's comrades, his change of heart till he blesses the water-snakes because he has come to love all living things, and the intervention of the polar spirits. That the marvellous story is presented with such rapidity and vividness helps to make it plausible; and, for once, Coleridge presents his story completely. *The Ancient Mariner* is Coleridge's only narrative poem which is not a fragment.

There is another factor in the speed of the narrative beside its brevity, and its exclusion of all but the most telling details. This is the manner in which the story is told by scenes, by events unfolded pictorially, somewhat in the manner of the cinematograph, rather than by narrative proper. Coleridge composed in the manner of the painter and the musician more than in the manner of the writer. The poem is all pictures as it passes before our eyes. Some of the most salient are the opening scene, where the Mariner holds the Wedding Guest against his will, the fog and ice scenes, the hideous figures on the phantom ship, the colored water-snakes, the phosphorescent lights on the water, and the seraph spirits standing on the dead bodies of the crew. Coleridge had a rich sense of color and light and he had the power to dream these scenes vividly. He spends no long space on a scene, but with a few clear details he makes it so vivid that the poem, like a cinematograph narrative, is remembered by scenes rather than by events.

Use of " Atmosphere " and Contrast.—*The Ancient Mariner*, like *Kubla Khan* and the First Part of *Christabel*, well exhibits Coleridge's gift of creating a strange or unusual atmosphere in which to enshroud the scenes and events of his narrative. He sees things in an unusual way, sometimes vividly but in a spectral light, as ghastly mist-forms, or through an opaline haze. Beside the special atmosphere of which Coleridge makes use, he relies also, in a distinctive way, upon the principle of contrast. The events themselves produce horror and dread, but he enhances this effect by the atmosphere which he throws about them, and by his telling use of contrasts of motion, and sound, and scene. Illustration may be found in the alternation of the violent, abnormal scenes when the storm strikes the ship in Part I with the scenes of stillness and rest as the calm comes upon it in Part II. The Mariner's sleep comes as a " relief motive," after the preceding excitement, at the opening of Part V. The ethereal motion of the ship in its homeward voyage affords another passage of quiet after violence. Similarly, the noises and groans following the Mariner's waking from his sleep are succeeded by the sweet musical sounds that he hears at dawn. In general, Coleridge follows an acceleration of the imagination of his readers, in this poem, by retard or cessation. There is contrast, too, in the pictures of the poem. Here and there through its spectral light come passages of vivid color, as when we are told of the lights on the sea at night, or of the colored water-snakes; though the colors used are few, they are abruptly contrasting and are unforgettable. And at intervals in the Mariner's narrative of life in mid-ocean, with its storm and calm, its violence and rest, its *incredible happenings*, we are brought back to the wedding

The Ancient Mariner

feast on land, its events, people, and music. This is one of the strongest contrasts of all, and one of the most telling of the poet's many devices for breaking the monotony of the narrative.

Another factor in the uniqueness of the poem is the variety which is afforded by unexpected changes in stanza, meter, and rhyme, introduced with telling abruptness, yet with the effect of complete artlessness. The poem has little or no character interest. Its "human" side is unusually slight. The reader sees and feels the story, but he is never made to pause for the portrayal or analysis of character.

Moral of the Poem.—*The Ancient Mariner* is the story of the liberation of the human soul, through love, from the bonds of indifference and passion. The stress is not placed upon the incidents themselves, but upon their workings on the soul of the central character. After killing the good bird, the Mariner is isolated from the world of human beings and spirits until he feels a reversal of heart. He who had been indifferent to life comes to love even the water-snakes, because they are alive; and his love of living things saves him. At the end he is thankful for the gift of life of which he was willing to rob the albatross. The poem has probably no ruling central idea. It is a phantasy. It moves in a dream world, and its appeal is made to the imagination and to the sense of beauty more than to the conscience. Too heavy a didactic hand should not be laid upon it. Coleridge himself has told us that it should not be given a moral meaning[*]—something which seemed essential to Wordsworth.

Nevertheless, as a sort of undertone, the poem does have moral meaning. The gain in depth and weight brought by the presence of a spiritual element is made clear if we try to think of the difference were it absent—as absent as it is from *Kubla Khan*, which has no meaning in the moral world at all. The general teaching is that of kindness toward man

---

[*] Appendix, p. 136.

The Ancient Mariner

and bird and beast; but literalness of interpretation, or insistence upon logic are out of place, in a consideration of Coleridge's dream-phantasy. Various critics have pointed out that the consequences are disproportionate to the crime, and that the heaviest punishment falls upon the innocent. The comrades of the slayer die of thirst and starvation, while the culprit is the only one of the crew to be saved. But the " lessons " to be derived from the poem are general, rather than literal or specific. It leaves, more or less consciously with the reader, a sense of these things: of the duty of kindness to animals, of the happiness of human companionship, of God's mercifulness toward the repentant, of the salvation of the human being through love of living things, and of the blessedness of prayer, as a manifestation of thankfulness and love.

Form.—*The Ancient Mariner* derives its form from the long narrative ballad of tradition, made popular by Bishop Percy's *Reliques of Ancient English Poetry*, published in 1765. In Coleridge's day, people were intensely interested in these pieces. *The Ancient Mariner* is in " fyts " or parts like *The Battle of Otterbourne*, or some of the *Robin Hood* ballads, and its stanza is the normal ballad stanza of four lines, as this from *Sir Patrick Spens*:

>The king sits in Dumferling towne,
> Drinking the blude-red wine;
>" O whar will I get guid sailor,
> To sail this ship of mine? "

Sometimes, as in the ballads, the normal quatrain stanza is swelled to six lines, or doubled to eight. In one case a stanza of nine lines occurs. Specifically, 106 of the 142 stanzas of the poem are normal four-line stanzas. The modifications introduced by the poet follow some change in the character of the narrative or of the feeling. Rhyme appears, as in the traditional ballads, at the end of the second and fourth lines; sometimes also at the end of the first and third; and occasionally there is inner rhyme. As regards rhythm, the basic *ballad lines*—alternating four and three stresses, and show-

The Ancient Mariner

ing irregular syllabification—are regularized into iambic tetrameter and trimeter, as—

> And now there came both mist and snow
> And it grew wondrous cold

$$\times\acute{}|\times\acute{}|\times\acute{}|\times\acute{}$$
$$\times\acute{}|\times\acute{}|\times\acute{}$$

Occasionally a trochee is substituted for an iamb, as—

> Nodding their heads before her goes

$$\acute{}\times|\times\acute{}|\times\acute{}|\times\acute{}$$

Or an anapæst is substituted for an iamb, as—

> By thy long gray beard and glittering eye

$$\times\times\acute{}|\times\acute{}|\times\acute{}|\times\times\acute{}$$

When Coleridge introduces divergencies from the regularized ballad stanza he does so with infallible skill, following some transition in the story or in the mood; and the effect of simplicity is always preserved. Occasionally he uses the ballad mannerism of question and answer; and sometimes, in the ballad fashion, he allows a light accent to rest on the final syllable of a word having properly initial accent.

> The Wedding Guest he beat his breast,
> Yet he cannot choose but hear;
> And thus spake on that ancient man,
> The bright-eyed Marinér.

The ballad liking for alliteration is also made use of. Coleridge makes the oral side of the poem no less a factor in its memorableness than the vivid power of the narrative. He does this by the many devices through which he varies the monotony of his handling, by the apparent artlessness of the expression, and by the subtlety of the musical effects he achieves.

The Ancient Mariner

The language is somewhat but not conspicuously archaic. In the first edition it was extremely archaic in both vocabulary and spelling. This mannerism was reduced by the poet, in a later reprinting, with much consequent gain; for it clogged the reading when present so abundantly. In the later form of the poem the archaic quality consists less in spelling than in the presence of a few old words—*wist, eftsoons, ken, uprist, swound, trow, thorough* for *through, Line* for *equator, Rime* for *Rhyme*. A glance at some of the omitted or modified lines, as cited in the notes, will make clear how many old forms or spellings—like *Ancyent, y-spread, withouten, ne* for *not*, etc.—were discarded.

Influence.—Unlike many poems of this period, notably Byron's and the verse-romances of Scott, *The Ancient Mariner* exercised no influence and won no popularity in Europe. Poems of the weird supernatural were no novelty for continental literature, and the narrative artlessness and simplicity of its manner did not appeal to foreign as to English readers. In England, too, at first, the poem was received without enthusiasm. Even Southey and Wordsworth felt dubious about it; its friendliest reader was Charles Lamb. But this stage was soon left behind, and *The Ancient Mariner* has remained the monument, *par excellence*, for England, of the "Ballad Revival." Parodies of it soon multiplied, a sure sign that a piece has won public attention. It was the progenitor of a long line of nineteenth century literary and romantic ballads. *The Ancient Mariner* was first in the field now occupied by poems like Keats's *La Belle Dame Sans Merci*, Rossetti's *Sister Helen* and *Stratton Water, The King's Tragedy, The White Ship,* Tennyson's *Lady Clare, The Sisters,* Swinburne's *The Bloody Son, The Witch Mother,* Longfellow's *The Wreck of the Hesperus, The Skeleton in Armor*. On the oral side, its influence was strong also. Coleridge's gift of weird melody, as well as his love for the weird supernatural, left traces on the verse of Scott, the ballads of Mrs. Browning, and on the verse of Rossetti, Lowell, and especially of Poe.

BIBLIOGRAPHICAL NOTE

BIOGRAPHIES of Coleridge have been written by James Gillman (vol. I only published), 1838; H. D. Traill, *English Men of Letters* series, 1884; Hall Caine, *Great Writers* series, 1887; and J. Dykes Campbell, 1894. Coleridge's *Letters* have been edited in 2 vols. by E. H. Coleridge, 1895.

The more important editions of Coleridge's poetry are the Pickering edition, 3 vols., 1834; and those edited by J. Dykes Campbell, 1893, and E. H. Coleridge, 1912.

Leading essays on Coleridge's poetry appear in the following: J. C. Shairp, *Studies in Poetry and Philosophy*, 1868; A. C. Swinburne, *Essays and Studies*, 1875; E. Dowden, *Studies in Literature*, 1878; Leslie Stephen, *Hours in a Library*, 1879; Mrs. Oliphant, *The Literary History of England in the End of the Eighteenth and Beginning of the Nineteenth Century*, I, vii, 1882; A Brandl, *Coleridge and the English Romantic School*, Berlin, 1886; J. R. Lowell, *Democracy and Other Addresses*, 1887; Walter Pater, *Appreciations*, 1889; A. E. Hancock, *The French Revolution and the English Poets*, 1899; G. E. Woodbury, *Makers of Literature*, 1900; R. Garnett, *Essays of an Ex-Librarian*, 1901; H. A. Beers, *English Romanticism in the XIX Century*, 1901; George Brandes, *Main Currents of Nineteenth Century Literature*, IV, English translation, 1905; W. J. Courthope, *History of English Poetry*, VI, 1910; *Cambridge History of English Literature*, XI, 1914; Oliver Elton, *A Survey of English Literature: 1780–1830*, II, 1912.

For *The Ancient Mariner* and *Christabel*, see also Charlotte A. Porter, and Eleanor P. Hammond in *Poet Lore*, VI, 1894, and X, 1898.

A Bibliography of Samuel Taylor Coleridge, by John Lewis Haney, was published in 1903.

THE RIME OF THE ANCIENT MARINER

IN SEVEN PARTS

> Facile credo, plures esse Naturas invisibiles quam visibiles in rerum universitate. Sed horum omnium familiam quis nobis enarrabit? et gradus et cognationes et discrimina et singulorum munera? Quid agunt? quae loca habitant? Harum rerum notitiam semper ambivit ingenium humanum, nunquam attigit. Iuvat, interea, non diffiteor, quandoque in animo, tanquam in tabula, maioris et melioris mundi imaginem contemplari: ne mens assuefacta hodiernae vitae minutiis se contrahat nimis, et tota subsidat in pusillas cogitationes. Sed veritati interea invigilandum est, modusque servandus, ut certa ab incertis, diem a nocte, distinguamus.
> T. BURNET: *Archæologiæ Philosophicæ*, p. 68.

I CAN readily believe that there are more invisible than visible beings in the universe. But who shall tell us the relationship of them all, their gradations, their resemblances, their distinguishing features, and their excellencies? What is their purpose? What is their abiding place? Human thought has always endeavored to gain this knowledge, but has never attained it. In the meantime, it helps, I think, to behold sometimes in the imagination, as in a picture, the vision of a greater and better world, lest the mind accustomed to the details of daily life become too restricted and become wholly absorbed in petty thoughts. We must ever be watchful for the truth, and must preserve our sense of moderation, that we may distinguish the certain from the uncertain, the day from the night.

The Rime of the Ancient Mariner

Part the First

I

<small>An ancient Mariner meeteth three Gallants bidden to a wedding-feast, and detaineth one.</small>

It is an ancient Mariner,
  And he stoppeth one of three.
"By thy long gray beard and glittering eye,
  Now wherefore stopp'st thou me?

II

" The Bridegroom's doors are opened wide,   5
  And I am next of kin;
The guests are met, the feast is set:
  May'st hear the merry din."

III

He holds him with his skinny hand;
  " There was a ship," quoth he.   10
" Hold off! unhand me, gray-beard loon! "
  Eftsoons his hand dropt he.

IV

<small>The Wedding-Guest is spellbound by the eye of the old seafaring man, and constrained to hear his tale.</small>

He holds him with his glittering eye—
  The Wedding-Guest stood still,
And listens like a three years' child: 15
  The Mariner hath his will.

V

The Wedding-Guest sat on a stone:
  He cannot choose but hear;
And thus spake on that ancient man,
  The bright-eyed Mariner.   20

The Rime of the Ancient Mariner

VI

"The ship was cheered, the harbour cleared;
  Merrily did we drop
Below the kirk, below the hill,
  Below the lighthouse top.

VII

The Sun came up upon the left, 25
  Out of the sea came he!
And he shone bright, and on the right
  Went down into the sea.

The Mariner tells how the ship sailed southward with a good wind and fair weather, till it reached the Line.

VIII

Higher and higher every day,
  Till over the mast at noon—" 30
The Wedding-Guest here beat his breast,
  For he heard the loud bassoon.

IX

The bride hath paced into the hall,
  Red as a rose is she;
Nodding their heads before her goes 35
  The merry minstrelsy.

The Wedding-Guest heareth the bridal music; but the Mariner continueth his tale.

X

The Wedding-Guest he beat his breast,
  Yet he cannot choose but hear;
And thus spake on that ancient man,
  The bright-eyed Mariner. 40

XI

"And now the Storm-Blast came, and he
  Was tyrannous and strong:
He struck with his o'ertaking wings,
  And chased us south along.

The ship driven by a storm toward the South Pole.

The Rime of the Ancient Mariner
XII

With sloping masts and dipping prow,   45
As who pursued with yell and blow
Still treads the shadow of his foe,
    And forward bends his head,
The ship drove fast, loud roared the blast,
    And southward aye we fled.   50

XIII

And now there came both mist and snow,
    And it grew wondrous cold:
And ice, mast-high, came floating by,
    As green as emerald.

XIV

The land of ice, and of fearful sounds, where no living thing was to be seen.

And through the drifts the snowy clifts   55
    Did send a dismal sheen:
Nor shapes of men nor beasts we ken—
    The ice was all between.

XV

The ice was here, the ice was there,
    The ice was all around: 60
It cracked and growled, and roared and howled,
    Like noises in a swound!

XVI

Till a great sea-bird, called the Albatross, came through the

At length did cross an Albatross,
    Thorough the fog it came;
As if it had been a Christian soul,   65
    We hailed it in God's name.

The Rime of the Ancient Mariner

XVII

It ate the food it ne'er had eat,
  And round and round it flew.
The ice did split with a thunder-fit;
  The helmsman steered us through!   70

snow-fog, and was received with great joy and hospitality.

XVIII

And a good south wind sprung up behind;
  The Albatross did follow,
And every day, for food or play,
  Came to the mariners' hollo!

And lo! the Albatross proveth a bird of good omen, and followeth the ship as it returned northward through fog and floating ice.

XIX

In mist or cloud, on mast or shroud,   75
  It perched for vespers nine;
Whiles all the night, through fog-smoke white,
  Glimmered the white moon-shine."

XX

" God save thee, ancient Mariner!
  From the fiends, that plague thee thus!—   80
Why look'st thou so? "—" With my cross-bow
  I shot the Albatross."

The ancient Mariner inhospitably killeth the pious bird of good omen.

PART THE SECOND

XXI

The Sun now rose upon the right:
  Out of the sea came he,
Still hid in mist, and on the left   85
  Went down into the sea.

The Rime of the Ancient Mariner

XXII

And the good south wind still blew behind,
    But no sweet bird did follow,
Nor any day, for food or play,
    Came to the mariners' hollo!   90

XXIII

His shipmates cry out against the ancient Mariner, for killing the bird of good luck.

And I had done a hellish thing,
    And it would work 'em woe:
For all averred, I had killed the bird
    That made the breeze to blow.
'Ah, wretch!' said they, 'the bird to slay, 95
    That made the breeze to blow!'

XXIV

But when the fog cleared off, they justify the same, and thus make themselves accomplices in the crime.

Nor dim nor red, like God's own head,
    The glorious Sun uprist:
Then all averred, I had killed the bird
    That brought the fog and mist.   100
''Twas right,' said they, 'such birds to slay,
    That bring the fog and mist.'

XXV

The fair breeze continues; the ship enters the Pacific Ocean and sails northward, even till it reaches the Line.

The fair breeze blew, the white foam flew,
    The furrow followed free:
We were the first that ever burst   105
    Into that silent sea.

XXVI

The ship hath been suddenly becalmed.

Down dropt the breeze, the sails dropt down,
    'Twas sad as sad could be;
And we did speak only to break
    The silence of the sea!   110

The Rime of the Ancient Mariner

XXVII

All in a hot and copper sky,
  The bloody Sun, at noon,
Right up above the mast did stand,
  No bigger than the Moon.

XXVIII

Day after day, day after day,   115
  We stuck, nor breath nor motion;
As idle as a painted ship
  Upon a painted ocean.

XXIX

Water, water, every where,
  And all the boards did shrink;   120   *And the Albatross begins to be avenged.*
Water, water, every where,
  Nor any drop to drink.

XXX

The very deep did rot: O Christ!
  That ever this should be!
Yea, slimy things did crawl with legs   125
  Upon the slimy sea.

XXXI

About, about, in reel and rout
  The death-fires danced at night;
The water, like a witch's oils,
  Burnt green, and blue, and white.   130

The Rime of the Ancient Mariner

XXXII

<small>A Spirit had followed them; one of the invisible inhabitants of this planet, neither departed souls</small>
And some in dreams assuréd were
   Of the Spirit that plagued us so:
Nine fathoms deep he had followed us
   From the land of mist and snow.

<small>nor angels; concerning whom the learned Jew, Josephus, and the Platonic Constantinopolitan, Michael Psellus, may be consulted. They are very numerous, and there is no climate or element without one or more.</small>

XXXIII

And every tongue, through utter drought,   135
   Was withered at the root;
<small>The shipmates in their sore distress would fain throw the whole guilt on the ancient Mariner: in sign whereof they hang the dead sea-bird round his neck.</small>
We could not speak, no more than if
   We had been choked with soot.

XXXIV

Ah! well-a-day! what evil looks
   Had I from old and young!   140
Instead of the cross, the Albatross
   About my neck was hung.

PART THE THIRD

XXXV

There passed a weary time. Each throat
   Was parched, and glazed each eye.
A weary time! a weary time!   145
   How glazed each weary eye,
<small>The ancient Mariner beholdeth a sign in the element afar off.</small>
When looking westward, I beheld
   A something in the sky.

XXXVI

At first it seemed a little speck,
   And then it seemed a mist;   150
It moved and moved, and took at last
   A certain shape, I wist.

The Rime of the Ancient Mariner

XXXVII

A speck, a mist, a shape, I wist!
  And still it neared and neared:
As if it dodged a water-sprite,   155
  It plunged and tacked and veered.

XXXVIII

With throats unslaked, with black lips baked,   *At its nearer approach, it seemeth him to be a ship; and at a dear ransom he freeth his speech from the bonds of thirst.*
  We could nor laugh nor wail;
Through utter drought all dumb we stood!
I bit my arm, I sucked the blood,   160
  And cried, A sail! a sail!

XXXIX

With throats unslaked, with black lips baked,
  Agape they heard me call:
Gramercy! they for joy did grin,   *A flash of joy.*
And all at once their breath drew in,   165
  As they were drinking all.

XL

See! see! (I cried) she tacks no more!   *And horror follows. For can it be a ship that comes onward without wind or tide?*
  Hither to work us weal;
Without a breeze, without a tide,
  She steadies with upright keel!   170

XLI

The western wave was all a-flame;
  The day was well-nigh done!
Almost upon the western wave
  Rested the broad bright Sun;
When that strange shape drove suddenly   175
  Betwixt us and the Sun.

The Rime of the Ancient Mariner

XLII

<small>It seemeth him but the skeleton of a ship.</small>

And straight the Sun was flecked with bars
   (Heaven's Mother send us grace!)
As if through a dungeon-grate he peered,
   With broad and burning face.   180

XLIII

Alas! (thought I, and my heart beat loud,)
   How fast she nears and nears!
Are those *her* sails that glance in the Sun,
   Like restless gossameres?

XLIV

<small>And its ribs are seen as bars on the face of the setting Sun.</small>

Are those *her* ribs through which the Sun   185
   Did peer as through a grate?

<small>The Spectre-Woman and her Death-mate, and no other on board the skeleton-ship.</small>

And is that Woman all her crew?
Is that a Death? and are there two?
   Is Death that Woman's mate?

XLV

<small>Like vessel, like crew!</small>

Her lips were red, her looks were free,   190
   Her locks were yellow as gold:
Her skin was as white as leprosy,
The Night-mare Life-in-Death was she,
   Who thicks man's blood with cold.

XLVI

<small>Death and Life-in-Death have diced for the ship's crew, and she (the latter) winneth the ancient Mariner.</small>

The naked hulk alongside came,   195
   And the twain were casting dice;
'The game is done! I've won, I've won!'
   Quoth she, and whistles thrice.

The Rime of the Ancient Mariner

XLVII

The Sun's rim dips; the stars rush out:
  At one stride comes the dark;
With far-heard whisper, o'er the sea,
  Off shot the spectre-bark.

200 — No twilight within the courts of the Sun.

XLVIII

We listened and looked sideways up!
Fear at my heart, as at a cup,
  My life-blood seemed to sip!
The stars were dim, and thick the night,
The steersman's face by his lamp gleamed white;
  From the sails the dew did drip—
Till clomb above the eastern bar
The hornéd Moon, with one bright star
  Within the nether tip.

205, 210 — At the rising of the Moon,

XLIX

One after one, by the star-dogged Moon,
  Too quick for groan or sigh,
Each turned his face with a ghastly pang,
  And cursed me with his eye.

215 — One after another,

L

Four times fifty living men,
  (And I heard nor sigh nor groan)
With heavy thump, a lifeless lump,
  They dropped down one by one.

His shipmates drop down dead;

LI

The souls did from their bodies fly,—
  They fled to bliss or woe!
And every soul it passed me by,
  Like the whizz of my cross-bow! "

220 — But Life-in-Death begins her work on the ancient Mariner.

The Rime of the Ancient Mariner

Part the Fourth

LII

The Wedding-Guest feareth that a Spirit is talking to him;

"I fear thee, ancient Mariner!
 I fear thy skinny hand!
And thou art long, and lank, and brown,
 As is the ribbed sea-sand.

LIII

"I fear thee, and thy glittering eye,
 And thy skinny hand, so brown."—

But the ancient Mariner assureth him of his bodily life, and proceedeth to relate his horrible penance.

"Fear not, fear not, thou Wedding-Guest!
 This body dropt not down.

LIV

Alone, alone, all, all alone,
 Alone on a wide, wide sea!
And never a saint took pity on
 My soul in agony.

LV

He despiseth the creatures of the calm,

The many men, so beautiful!
 And they all dead did lie:
And a thousand thousand slimy things
 Lived on; and so did I.

LVI

And envieth that they should live, and so many lie dead.

I looked upon the rotting sea,
 And drew my eyes away;
I looked upon the rotting deck,
 And there the dead men lay.

LVII

I looked to heaven, and tried to pray;
 But or ever a prayer had gusht,
A wicked whisper came, and made
 My heart as dry as dust.

The Rime of the Ancient Mariner

LVIII

I closed my lids, and kept them close,
   And the balls like pulses beat;
For the sky and the sea, and the sea and the sky
Lay like a load on my weary eye,   251
   And the dead were at my feet.

LIX

The cold sweat melted from their limbs,
   Nor rot nor reek did they:
The look with which they looked on me   255
   Had never passed away.

But the curse liveth for him in the eye of the dead men.

LX

An orphan's curse would drag to Hell
   A spirit from on high;
But oh! more horrible than that
   Is a curse in a dead man's eye!   260
Seven days, seven nights, I saw that curse,
   And yet I could not die.

LXI

The moving Moon went up the sky,
   And nowhere did abide:
Softly she was going up,   265
   And a star or two beside—

LXII

Her beams bemocked the sultry main
   Like April hoar-frost spread;
But where the ship's huge shadow lay,
The charmèd water burnt alway   270
   A still and awful red.

In his loneliness and fixedness he yearneth towards the journeying Moon, and the stars that still sojourn, yet still move onward; and everywhere the blue sky belongs to them, and is their appointed rest, and their native country and their own natural homes, which they enter unannounced, as lords that are certainly expected and yet there is a silent joy at their arrival.

The Rime of the Ancient Mariner

LXIII

By the light of the Moon he beholdeth God's creatures of the great calm.

Beyond the shadow of the ship,
   I watched the water-snakes:
They moved in tracks of shining white,
And when they reared, the elfish light   275
   Fell off in hoary flakes.

LXIV

Within the shadow of the ship
   I watched their rich attire:
Blue, glossy green, and velvet black,
They coiled and swam; and every track   280
   Was a flash of golden fire.

LXV

Their beauty and their happiness.

O happy living things! no tongue
   Their beauty might declare:
A spring of love gushed from my heart,

He blesseth them in his heart.

And I blessed them unaware: 285
Sure my kind saint took pity on me,
   And I blessed them unaware:

LXVI

The spell begins to break.

The selfsame moment I could pray;
   And from my neck so free
The Albatross fell off, and sank   290
   Like lead into the sea.

Part the Fifth

LXVII

Oh sleep! it is a gentle thing,
   Beloved from pole to pole!
To Mary Queen the praise be given!
She sent the gentle sleep from Heaven,   295
   That slid into my soul.

The Rime of the Ancient Mariner

LXVIII

The silly buckets on the deck,   *By grace of
  That had so long remained,   the holy
I dreamt that they were filled with dew;   *Mother, the ancient
  And when I awoke, it rained.   300 Mariner is refreshed with rain.*

LXIX

My lips were wet, my throat was cold,
  My garments all were dank;
Sure I had drunken in my dreams,
  And still my body drank.

LXX

I moved, and could not feel my limbs: 305
  I was so light—almost
I thought that I had died in sleep,
  And was a blessèd ghost.

LXXI

And soon I heard a roaring wind: *He heareth
  It did not come anear;   310 sounds and seeth strange
But with its sound it shook the sails,   sights and commotions
  That were so thin and sere.   in the sky and the element.*

LXXII

The upper air burst into life!
  And a hundred fire-flags sheen,
To and fro they were hurried about!   315
And to and fro, and in and out,
  The wan stars danced between.

LXXIII

And the coming wind did roar more loud,
  And the sails did sigh like sedge;
And the rain poured down from one black cloud;
  The Moon was at its edge.   321

The Rime of the Ancient Mariner

LXXIV

The thick black cloud was cleft, and still
  The Moon was at its side:
Like waters shot from some high crag,
The lightning fell with never a jag,   325
  A river steep and wide.

LXXV

The bodies of the ship's crew are inspirited and the ship moves on;

The loud wind never reached the ship,
  Yet now the ship moved on!
Beneath the lightning and the Moon
  The dead men gave a groan.   330

LXXVI

They groaned, they stirred, they all uprose,
  Nor spake, nor moved their eyes;
It had been strange, even in a dream,
  To have seen those dead men rise.

LXXVII

The helmsman steered, the ship moved on;   335
  Yet never a breeze up blew;
The mariners all 'gan work the ropes,
  Where they were wont to do;
They raised their limbs like lifeless tools—
  We were a ghastly crew.   340

LXXVIII

The body of my brother's son
  Stood by me, knee to knee:
The body and I pulled at one rope,
  But he said nought to me."

The Rime of the Ancient Mariner

LXXIX

"I fear thee, ancient Mariner!"   345
  "Be calm, thou Wedding-Guest!
'Twas not those souls that fled in pain,
Which to their corses came again,
  But a troop of spirits blest:

But not by the souls of the men, nor by dæmons of earth or middle air, but by a blessed troop of angelic spirits, sent down by the invocation of the guardian saint.

LXXX

For when it dawned—they dropped their arms,
  And clustered round the mast;   351
Sweet sounds rose slowly through their mouths,
  And from their bodies passed.

LXXXI

Around, around, flew each sweet sound,
  Then darted to the Sun;   355
Slowly the sounds came back again,
  Now mixed, now one by one.

LXXXII

Sometimes a-dropping from the sky
  I heard the sky-lark sing;
Sometimes all little birds that are,   360
How they seemed to fill the sea and air
  With their sweet jargoning!

LXXXIII

And now 'twas like all instruments,
  Now like a lonely flute;
And now it is an angel's song,   365
  That makes the heavens be mute.

LXXXIV

It ceased: yet still the sails made on
  A pleasant noise till noon,
A noise like of a hidden brook

The Rime of the Ancient Mariner

In the leafy month of June,   370
That to the sleeping woods all night
Singeth a quiet tune.

LXXXV

Till noon we quietly sailed on,
  Yet never a breeze did breathe:
Slowly and smoothly went the ship,   375
  Moved onward from beneath.

LXXXVI

The lonesome Spirit from the South-Pole carries on the ship as far as the Line, in obedience to the angelic troop, but still requireth vengeance.

Under the keel nine fathom deep,
  From the land of mist and snow,
The spirit slid: and it was he
  That made the ship to go.   380
The sails at noon left off their tune,
  And the ship stood still also.

LXXXVII

The Sun, right up above the mast,
  Had fixed her to the ocean:
But in a minute she 'gan stir,   385
  With a short uneasy motion—
Backwards and forwards half her length
  With a short uneasy motion.

LXXXVIII

Then like a pawing horse let go,
  She made a sudden bound;   390
It flung the blood into my head,
  And I fell down in a swound.

LXXXIX

How long in that same fit I lay,
  I have not to declare;
But ere my living life returned,   395
I heard and in my soul discerned
  Two voices in the air.

The Rime of the Ancient Mariner

XC

'Is it he?' quoth one, 'Is this the man?
  By him who died on cross,
With his cruel bow he laid full low,   400
  The harmless Albatross.

XCI

The spirit who bideth by himself
  In the land of mist and snow,
He loved the bird that loved the man
Who shot him with his bow.'   405

The Polar Spirit's fellow-dæmon, the invisible inhabitants of the element, take part in his wrong; and two of them relate, one to the other, that penance long and heavy for the ancient Mariner hath been accorded to the Polar Spirit, who returneth southward.

XCII

The other was a softer voice,
  As soft as honey-dew:
Quoth he, 'The man hath penance done,
  And penance more will do.'

Part the Sixth

XCIII

FIRST VOICE

'But tell me, tell me! speak again,   410
  Thy soft response renewing—
What makes that ship drive on so fast?
  What is the Ocean doing?'

XCIV

SECOND VOICE

'Still as a slave before his lord,
  The Ocean hath no blast.   415
His great bright eye most silently
  Up to the Moon is cast—

The Rime of the Ancient Mariner

XCV

If he may know which way to go;
  For she guides him smooth or grim.
See, brother, see! how graciously   420
  She looketh down on him.'

XCVI

FIRST VOICE

The Mariner hath been cast into a trance; for the angelic power causeth the vessel to drive northward faster than human life could endure.

But why drives on that ship so fast,
  Without or wave or wind? '

SECOND VOICE

' The air is cut away before,
  And closes from behind.   425

XCVII

Fly, brother, fly! more high, more high!
  Or we shall be belated:
For slow and slow that ship will go,
  When the Mariner's trance is abated.'

XCVIII

The supernatural motion is retarded; the Mariner awakes, and his penance begins anew.

I woke, and we were sailing on   430
  As in a gentle weather:
'Twas night, calm night, the Moon was high;
  The dead men stood together.

XCIX

All stood together on the deck,
  For a charnel-dungeon fitter: 435
All fixed on me their stony eyes,
  That in the Moon did glitter.

The Rime of the Ancient Mariner

C

The pang, the curse, with which they died,
  Had never passed away:
I could not draw my eyes from theirs,   440
  Nor turn them up to pray.

CI

And now this spell was snapt: once more   *The curse is finally expiated.*
  I viewed the ocean green,
And looked far forth, yet little saw
  Of what had else been seen—   445

CII

Like one, that on a lonesome road
  Doth walk in fear and dread,
And having once turned round walks on,
  And turns no more his head;
Because he knows, a frightful fiend   450
  Doth close behind him tread.

CIII

But soon there breathed a wind on me,
  Nor sound nor motion made:
Its path was not upon the sea,
  In ripple or in shade.   455

CIV

It raised my hair, it fanned my cheek
  Like a meadow-gale of spring—
It mingled strangely with my fears,
  Yet it felt like a welcoming.

The Rime of the Ancient Mariner

CV

    Swiftly, swiftly flew the ship,   460
        Yet she sailed softly too:
    Sweetly, sweetly blew the breeze—
        On me alone it blew.

CVI

And the ancient Mariner beholdeth his native country.

    Oh! dream of joy! is this indeed
        The light-house top I see?   465
    Is this the hill? is this the kirk?
        Is this mine own countree?

CVII

    We drifted o'er the harbour-bar,
        And I with sobs did pray—
    O let me be awake, my God!   470
        Or let me sleep alway.

CVIII

    The harbour-bay was clear as glass,
        So smoothly it was strewn!
    And on the bay the moonlight lay,
        And the shadow of the Moon.   475

CVIX

    The rock shone bright, the kirk no less,
        That stands above the rock:
    The moonlight steeped in silentness
        The steady weathercock.

CX

The angelic spirits leave the dead

    And the bay was white with silent light,   480
        Till rising from the same,
    Full many shapes, that shadows were,
        In crimson colours came.

The Rime of the Ancient Mariner

CXI

A little distance from the prow
  Those crimson shadows were: 485 *And appear in their own forms of light.*
I turned my eyes upon the deck—
  Oh, Christ! what saw I there!

CXII

Each corse lay flat, lifeless and flat,
  And, by the holy rood!
A man all light, a seraph-man,   490
  On every corse there stood.

CXIII

This seraph-band, each waved his hand:
  It was a heavenly sight!
They stood as signals to the land,
  Each one a lovely light: 495

CXIV

This seraph-band, each waved his hand,
  Nor voice did they impart—
No voice; but oh! the silence sank
  Like music on my heart.

CXV

But soon I heard the dash of oars;   500
  I heard the Pilot's cheer;
My head was turned perforce away,
  And I saw a boat appear.

CXVI

The Pilot, and the Pilot's boy,
  I heard them coming fast: 505
Dear Lord in Heaven!·it was a joy
  The dead men could not blast.

The Rime of the Ancient Mariner

CXVII

I saw a third—I heard his voice:
   It is the Hermit good!
He singeth loud his godly hymns   510
   That he makes in the wood.
He'll shrieve my soul, he'll wash away
   The Albatross's blood.

Part the Seventh

CXVIII

The Hermit of the Wood   This Hermit good lives in that wood
   Which slopes down to the sea: 515
How loudly his sweet voice he rears!
He loves to talk with marineres
   That come from a far countree.

CXIX

He kneels at morn, and noon, and eve—
   He hath a cushion plump: 520
It is the moss that wholly hides
   The rotted old oak-stump.

CXX

The skiff-boat neared: I heard them talk,
   'Why this is strange, I trow!
Where are those lights so many and fair,   525
   That signal made but now?'

CXXI

Approacheth the ship with wonder.   'Strange, by my faith!' the Hermit said—
   'And they answered not our cheer!
The planks looked warped! and see those sails,
   How thin they are and sere!   530
I never saw aught like to them,
   Unless perchance it were

The Rime of the Ancient Mariner

CXXII

Brown skeletons of leaves that lag
  My forest-brook along;
When the ivy-tod is heavy with snow,   535
And the owlet whoops to the wolf below,
  That eats the she-wolf's young.'

CXXIII

' Dear Lord! it hath a fiendish look—
  (The Pilot made reply)
I am a-feared '—' Push on, push on! '   540
  Said the Hermit cheerily.

CXXIV

The boat came closer to the ship,
  But I nor spake nor stirred;
The boat came close beneath the ship,
  And straight a sound was heard.   545

CXXV

Under the water it rumbled on,   *The ship suddenly sinketh.*
  Still louder and more dread;
It reached the ship, it split the bay;
  The ship went down like lead.

CXXVI

Stunned by that loud and dreadful sound,   550   *The ancient Mariner is saved in the Pilot's boat.*
  Which sky and ocean smote,
Like one that hath been seven days drowned
  My body lay afloat;
But swift as dreams, myself I found
  Within the Pilot's boat.   555

CXXVII

Upon the whirl, where sank the ship,
  The boat spun round and round;
And all was still, save that the hill
  Was *telling of the* sound.

The Rime of the Ancient Mariner

CXXVIII

I moved my lips—the Pilot shrieked 560
    And fell down in a fit;
The holy Hermit raised his eyes,
    And prayed where he did sit.

CXXIX

I took the oars: the Pilot's boy,
    Who now doth crazy go, 565
Laughed loud and long, and all the while
    His eyes went to and fro.
'Ha! ha!' quoth he, 'full plain I see,
    The Devil knows how to row.'

CXXX

And now, all in my own countree, 570
    I stood on the firm land!
The Hermit stepped forth from the boat,
    And scarcely he could stand.

CXXXI

The ancient Mariner earnestly entreateth the Hermit to shrieve him; and the penance of life falls on him.

'O shrieve me, shrieve me, holy man!'
    The Hermit crossed his brow. 575
'Say quick,' quoth he, 'I bid thee say—
    What manner of man art thou?'

CXXXII

Forthwith this frame of mine was wrenched
    With a woful agony,
Which forced me to begin my tale; 580
    And then it left me free.

CXXXIII

And ever and anon throughout his future life an agony constraineth him to travel from land to land.

Since then, at an uncertain hour,
    That agony returns;
And till my ghastly tale is told,
    This heart within me burns. 585

The Rime of the Ancient Mariner

CXXXIV

I pass, like night, from land to land;
  I have strange power of speech;
That moment that his face I see,
  I know the man that must hear me:
    To him my tale I teach.   590

CXXXV

What loud uproar bursts from that door!
  The wedding-guests are there:
But in the garden-bower the bride
  And bride-maids singing are:
And hark the little vesper bell,   595
  Which biddeth me to prayer!

CXXXVI

O Wedding-Guest! this soul hath been
  Alone on a wide wide sea:
So lonely 'twas, that God himself
  Scarce seeméd there to be.   600

CXXXVII

O sweeter than the marriage-feast,
  'Tis sweeter far to me,
To walk together to the kirk
  With a goodly company!—

CXXXVIII

To walk together to the kirk,   605
  And all together pray
While each to his great Father bends,
Old men, and babes, and loving friends
  And youths and maidens gay!

The Rime of the Ancient Mariner

CXXXIX

And to teach, by his own example, love and reverence to all things that God made and loveth.

 Farewell, farewell, but this I tell   610
  To thee, thou Wedding-Guest!
 He prayeth well, who loveth well
  Both man and bird and beast.

CXL

 He prayeth best, who loveth best
  All things both great and small;   615
 For the dear God who loveth us,
  He made and loveth all."

CXLI

 The Mariner, whose eye is bright,
  Whose beard with age is hoar,
 Is gone: and now the Wedding-Guest   620
  Turned from the bridegroom's door.

CXLII

 He went like one that hath been stunned,
  And is of sense forlorn:
 A sadder and a wiser man,
  He rose the morrow morn.   625

INTRODUCTION TO CHRISTABEL AND KUBLA KHAN

CHRISTABEL

Composition and Publication.—The First Part of *Christabel* was written in 1797, in Coleridge's great creative year. The Second Part was composed in 1800, after a lapse of several years, in which he had visited Germany with the Wordsworths. It was intended for publication in the second edition of the *Lyrical Ballads*. Coleridge found himself unable to complete the poem, after composing the Second Part. It remains, like most of Coleridge's work, a fragment. It was circulated in manuscript form for some years. Scott heard it in 1808, Byron in 1811. Finally, on Byron's recommendation, it was published, in its unfinished state. In the preface Coleridge wrote: " But, as in my very first conception of the tale, I had the whole present to my mind, with the wholeness no less than the liveliness of a vision, I trust that I shall be able to embody in verse the three parts yet to come in the course of the present year." Later he said, " I could write as good verses now as ever I did, if I were perfectly free from vexations, and were I in the *ad libitum* hearing of fine music, which has a sensible effect in harmonizing my thoughts, and in animating and, as it were, lubricating my inventive faculty. The reason of my not finishing *Christabel*, is not that I don't know how to do it—for I have, as I always had, the whole plan entire from beginning to end in my mind; but I fear I could not carry on with equal success the execution of the idea, an extremely subtle and difficult one."[1]

Mr. Gillman has preserved a projected completion of the

---

[1] *Table Talk*, July 6, 1833.

Introduction to Christabel

tale, explained to him by Coleridge.[2] Regarding this projected completion, however, the report of Coleridge's nephew as to what was said to him by Wordsworth, in 1836, should be kept in mind: "He said he had no idea how *Christabel* was to have been finished, and he did not think my uncle had ever conceived, in his own mind, any definite plan for it; that the poem had been composed . . . when there was the most unreserved intercourse between them as to all their literary projects and productions, and he had never heard from him any plan for finishing it. Not that he doubted my uncle's sincerity in his subsequent assertions to the contrary; because, he said, schemes of this sort passed rapidly and vividly through his mind, and so impressed him that he often fancied he had arranged things which really, and upon trial, proved to be mere embryos.".[3] It was probably well that the poem was never finished. The level attained in the First Part, or even in the Second, could hardly have been maintained by Coleridge, and, in any case, it is less the narrative itself than its atmosphere and its unique melodies which have given the poem distinctive place.

As regards indebtedness for materials, Coleridge owes most to the mediæval verse romances, in this poem, just as in *The Ancient Mariner* he owes most to the ballads. He derives from them the form, a variation of the octosyllabic rhymed couplets of the poetic romances of the middle ages. Other features which he owes to them, or to his antiquarian interest, are his moated castle and iron-barred gate, his feudal barons, harpers, heralds, and pages, and the like. But there is no definite source for his material. One critic thinks a suggestion was taken from Mrs. Radcliffe's *Mysteries of Udolpho* (1794) and the general situation from the same author's *The Romance of the Forest* (1791), and that touches here and there were derived from Bürger's *Lenore*,

---

[2] Appendix, p. 136.
[3] *The Prose Works of William Wordsworth*, edited by A. B. Grosart, III, 427. 1876.

Introduction to Christabel

Lewis's *Alonzo the Brave and the Fair Imogene,* and from the ballads. But in no case is the debt, if there is one, very great. To these should be added, thinks another critic, the Melusina, or Greek Lamia myth, of a serpent-maiden, used a little later by Keats in his *Lamia,* written in 1818. Keats took his groundwork from the story in Burton's *Anatomy of Melancholy*[*] (1621), who in turn had it from Appolonius. Geraldine is the embodiment of pagan spirits lingering in mediæval woods; but while Keats makes his serpent-maiden attractive, until she enlists sympathy, Coleridge develops the repugnant side, and endows her with a motiveless malignity and a nameless dread.

The First and Second Parts Compared.—The isolation and mystery making credible impossible things, lent by the mid-ocean setting to *The Ancient Mariner,* is afforded by the dimly moonlit wood, and by midnight in the feudal castle, in *Christabel.* The spell of the First Part has been universally recognized. It helps that many of its suggestions are unsolved. A poem should contain the key to its own mysteries; but perhaps *Christabel* gains from the fact that Geraldine is never certainly explained to the reader. It remains futile to ask whether she is a sorceress, casting a malignant spell, or whether she only seems to do so to Christabel, in the fascination of her terror. The poet excites and suspends curiosity. There are many omens as to the malign character of Geraldine's presence. She sinks at the threshold, probably because it has been blessed by the church. She cannot praise the Virgin. The thought of Christabel's mother makes her ill at ease. The mastiff moans at her passing; animals are supposed to be conscious of the presence of supernatural beings. Even the fire seems to be aware of her, and darts out a tongue of flame. To Christabel she has the fascination of a snake, and the effect of her glittering eyes is that of a snake hypnotizing its victim. But all these sinister manifestations might be due to chance, or to her victim's terror. Did she utter the words of a spell? The

---
[*] III, 1, i.

Introduction to Christabel

poet does not say so directly. Christabel may have imagined it. We are not even certain as to the baleful mark she bore on her breast and half her side, whether it was the disfigurement of serpent's scales. It might have been an illusion caused by the shadow of the silver lamp. Coleridge made Geraldine a witch, in his projected conclusion of the poem; but we are not told definitely that she was a witch in the poem as we have it. The unsolved mysteries of the First Part seem to deepen its spell.

The Second Part is longer and has greater definiteness, but it is less successful. It contains more mediæval "properties" and more archaisms in language, but the composition is less spontaneous and the enchantment fades. In the three years that intervened before its composition, some of Coleridge's inspiration had vanished. The spectral light is lost, for the events of this part occur in daytime; and the definite localization is not of help but detracts. Place-names are sprinkled thickly throughout the Second Part. The castle is located nowhere in particular in the First Part; it exists in the poet's dreamland. It becomes "Langdale Hall" in the Second Part. References to Windermere, Borrowdale, Dungeon-ghyll, take the reader to Cumberland and the Lake country, the scene of most of Wordsworth's poems, a region not especially appropriate for a romantic story of the character of *Christabel*. The magic of suggestion, of expression, of music, fails somewhat. The tale becomes a simple tale of adventure, enchantment, and chivalry, a field wherein Scott, not Coleridge, is master. Judging from the lapse of the Second Part from the First, and bearing in mind the probable falling off of a possible Third and Fourth Part, it seems well, to most critics, that Coleridge did not try to continue.

The poem has no moral meaning. There is a haunting suggestion of deeper meanings, as of allegory; but no spiritual significance was intended, and none should be looked for. Coleridge himself said that it "pretended to be nothing more than a common fairy tale."[5]

---

[5] *Biographia Literaria*, Chapter XXIV.

Introduction to Christabel

Form.—If *The Ancient Mariner* is a ballad, *Christabel* is a metrical romance, or verse tale of chivalric adventure. The general novelty of the poem, in form no less than in matter, made a strong impression in Coleridge's day—an impression that may fairly be compared with that made by the novelty of " free " verse to-day. Basic is the eight-syllabled rhyming couplet, in iambic rhythm, of the mediæval verse romances. But Coleridge introduces many variations to give it richness and variety. He alternates couplet rhymes and triplets, introduces alternate rhymes and inner rhymes, breaks up his lines into irregular stanzas, uses the pause as a device in rhythm, and produces new cadences. The result was a wholly new style of versification, which had a strong influence upon nineteenth century prosody. Coleridge helped to restore the freedom of English verse, and he established virtually a new meter.

An example of the use of pause is afforded by the opening lines, where the third line occupies the same time as the preceding.

> 'Tis the middle of night by the castle clock,
> And the owls have awakened the crowing cock,
>   Tu—whit——Tu—whoo!
> And hark, again! the crowing cock!
>   How drowsily it crew.

The skilful introduction of anapæsts, suggesting excitement or hurry, dropping again to effects of retard or hush, when the iambic or trochaic movement is resumed, may be seen in passages like—

> They crossed the moat and Christabel
> Took the key that fitted well;
> A little door she opened straight,
> All in the middle of the gate;
> The gate that was ironed within and without,
> Where an army in battle array had marched out,
> The lady sank, belike through pain,
> And Christabel with might and main

Introduction to Christabel

> Lifted her up, a weary weight
> Over the threshold of the gate.
> Then the lady rose again,
> And moved as she were not in pain.

and this—

> They passed the hall that echoes still,
> Pass as lightly as you will!
> The brands were flat, the brands were dying,
> Amid their own white ashes lying;
> But when the lady passed there came
> A tongue of light, a fit of flame;
> And Christabel saw the lady's eye,
> And nothing else saw she thereby,
> Save the boss of the shield of Sir Leoline tall,
> Which hung in a murky old niche on the wall.
> "O softly tread," said Christabel.
> "My father seldom sleepeth well.'

Influence.—The influence of *Christabel* was very strong, not only of its subject-matter, and the form, but of single lines and images. The " light horseman " stanza employed by Scott in *The Lay of the Last Minstrel*, and in other verse romances, was assimilated by him from hearing part of *Christabel* recited, while it was still in manuscript form. He repeats in the *Lay* the line, " Jesu, Maria, shield her well." Scott's scene in the Second Canto, where Lady Margaret steals down out of Branksome Tower, at dawn, gliding down the secret stair, patting the bloodhound, and issuing through the postern to meet her knight under the trees, sounds as though derived from the opening scene of *Christabel*. Even where definite indebtedness cannot be pointed out, the general influence of the poem on succeeding verse is not to be denied. Its most immediate descendant was Keats's *Eve of St. Agnes,* in which Keats is even more richly pictorial than Coleridge. Here and there, the influence of Coleridge's manner, especially of his prosody, is to be felt in the poetry of Shelley, Mrs. Browning, Tennyson, Swinburne, and others.

Introduction to Kubla Khan

KUBLA KHAN

Composition of the Poem.—Coleridge has left this account of *Kubla Khan*, which was first published, with *Christabel* and *The Pains of Sleep*, in 1814:

In the summer of the year 1797, the author, then in ill health, had retired to a lonely farm-house between Porlock and Linton, on the Exmoor confines of Somerset and Devonshire. In consequence of a slight indisposition, an anodyne had been prescribed, from the effects of which he fell asleep in his chair at the moment that he was reading the following sentence, or words of the same substance, in Purchas's "Pilgrimage": "Here the Khan Kubla commanded a palace to be built, and a stately garden thereunto. And thus ten miles of fertile ground were inclosed with a wall." The author continued for about three hours in a profound sleep, at least of the external senses, during which time he has the most vivid confidence, that he could not have composed less than from two to three hundred lines; if that indeed can be called composition in which all the images rose up before him as *things,* with a parallel production of the correspondent expressions, without any sensation or consciousness of effort. On awaking he appeared to himself to have a distinct recollection of the whole, and, taking his pen, ink, and paper, instantly and eagerly wrote down the lines that are here preserved. At this moment he was unfortunately called out by a person on business from Porlock, and detained by him above an hour, and on his return to his room, found, to his no small surprise and mortification, that though he still retained some vague and dim recollection of the general purport of the vision, yet, with the exception of some eight or ten scattered lines and images, all the rest had passed away, like the images on the surface of a stream into which a stone has been cast, but, alas! without the after restoration of the latter . . . Yet from the still surviving recol-

Introduction to Kubla Khan

lections in his mind, the author has frequently purposed to finish for himself what had been originally, as it were, given to him . . . but the to-morrow is yet to come."[6]

Kubla Khan is then, literally, a dream poem. It was composed in sleep, and probably a not quite healthy but a narcotized sleep. The student may fairly compare it with its companion poem, *The Pains of Sleep*, composed when his dreams had assumed another character.

> But yester-night I prayed aloud
> In anguish and in agony, .
> Up-starting from the fiendish crowd
> Of shapes and thoughts that tortured me:
> A lurid light, a trampling throng.

In its lack of logical sequence of ideas, *Kubla Khan* illustrates, in extreme degree, the emancipation from the "common sense" of the eighteenth century. It is an excellent example of the mystery, strangeness, indefiniteness, characterizing the "romantic" in poetry. There enter into it records of oriental travel, descriptions of landscape, echoes of tales of romance and diablerie, and touches of folk-lore. These were taken up and fused by the author's imagination. They are poured forth in a succession of dream pictures, oriental in coloring, depicted in a stream of vivid imagery, and clothed in weird, romantic melody. The whole is fragmentary, charged with suggestion, varied, yet harmonious. It is as unfinished and shifting and impalpable as a dream.

Form.—The extreme fluidity and ease of the metrical movement are striking. Analysis of it reveals many subtle effects of acceleration and retard, accompanying transitions in the imagery. The poem starts with smooth iambic movement.—

> In Xanadu did Kubla Khan
> A stately pleasure dome decree

---

[6] *Coleridge's* note on the poem, 1814.

Introduction to Kubla Khan

Still iambic, but with hastened effect is—
> Through caverns measureless to man

Trochaic rhythm is substituted in—
> Down to a sunless sea.

Variation is afforded by occasional anapæsts like—
> And there | were gar|dens bright | with sin|uous rills,
>
> Five miles | mean|dering with | a ma|zy motion

And there are effects of retard, echoic in quality, which clog the movement, as—
> And from this chasm with ceaseless turmoil seething,
> As if this earth in fast thick pants were breathing,
> A mighty fountain momently was forced:

Besides end-rhyme variously arranged, in lines of varying length, the poet makes unusual and striking use of alliteration, and of *assonance,* or correspondence of vowel sounds. The " key " vowel sound of the poem appears in words like *Xanadu, Khan, Alph, caverns, romantic chasm, slanted, savage, chaffy, damsel.* The composition was unconscious, and there is no suggestion of the labored, or of deliberate selection. Yet it would be difficult to cite a poem in which such effective use is made of specific sounds, whether of soft-flowing liquids—*l*'s, *m*'s, *n*'s, *r*'s—or of fricatives—as *th*'s *s*'s, *f*'s—which hold back the movement. Coleridge is often cited by students of prosody as affording excellent illustration of the use a poet may make of the qualities of sound for the purpose of enhancing the melodiousness of verse, or of echoing the ideas to be conveyed by the sounds employed.

CHRISTABEL

Part the First

'Tis the middle of night by the castle clock,
And the owls have awakened the crowing cock;
  Tu-whit!—Tu-whoo!
And hark, again! the crowing cock,
  How drowsily it crew.

Sir Leoline, the Baron rich,
Hath a toothless mastiff bitch;
From her kennel beneath the rock
She maketh answer to the clock,
Four for the quarters, and twelve for the hour;
Ever and aye, by shine and shower,
Sixteen short howls, not over loud;
Some say, she sees my lady's shroud.

Is the night chilly and dark?
The night is chilly but not dark.
The thin gray cloud is spread on high,
It covers but not hides the sky.
The moon is behind, and at the full;
And yet she looks both small and dull.
The night is chill, the cloud is gray:
'Tis a month before the month of May,
And the Spring comes slowly up this way.

The lovely lady, Christabel,
Whom her father loves so well,
What makes her in the wood so late,
A furlong from the castle gate?
She had dreams all yesternight
Of her own betrothéd knight
And she in the midnight wood will pray
For the weal of her lover that's far away.

Christabel

She stole along, she nothing spoke,
The sighs she heaved were soft and low,
And naught was green upon the oak
But mosses and rarest mistletoe:
She kneels beneath the huge oak tree, 35
And in silence prayeth she.

The lady sprang up suddenly,
The lovely lady Christabel!
It moaned as near, as near can be,
But what it is she cannot tell. 40
On the other side it seems to be,
Of the huge broad-breasted, old oak tree.

The night is chill; the forest bare;
Is it the wind that moaneth bleak?
There is not wind enough in the air 45
To move away the ringlet curl
From the lovely lady's cheek—
There is not wind enough to twirl
The one red leaf, the last of its clan,
That dances as often as dance it can, 50
Hanging so light and hanging so high,
On the topmost twig that looks up at the sky.

Hush, beating heart of Christabel!
Jesu, Maria, shield her well!
She folded her arms beneath her cloak, 55
And stole to the other side of the oak.
     What sees she there?

There she sees a damsel bright,
Drest in a silken robe of white,
That shadowy in the moonlight shone: 60
The neck that made the white robe wan,
Her stately neck, and arms were bare;
Her blue-veined feet unsandal'd were,
And wildly glittered here and there

Christabel

The gems entangled in her hair. 65
I guess, 'twas frightful there to see
A lady so richly clad as she—
Beautiful exceedingly!

" Mary mother, save me now! "
(Said Christabel) " And who art thou? " 70

The lady strange made answer meet,
And her voice was faint and sweet:—
" Have pity on my sore distress;
I scarce can speak for weariness:
Stretch forth thy hand and have no fear! " 75
Said Christabel, " How camest thou here? "
And the lady, whose voice was faint and sweet,
Did thus pursue her answer meet:—

" My sire is of a noble line,
And my name is Geraldine: 80
Five warriors seized me yestermorn,
Me, even me, a maid forlorn:
They choked my cries with force and fright,
And tied me on a palfrey white.
The palfrey was as fleet as wind, 85
And they rode furiously behind.
They spurred amain, their steeds were white:
And once we crossed the shade of night.
As sure as Heaven shall rescue me,
I have no thought what men they be; 90
Nor do I know how long it is
(For I have lain entranced, I wis)
Since one, the tallest of the five,
Took me from the palfrey's back,
A weary woman, scarce alive. 95
Some muttered words his comrades spoke:
He placed me underneath this oak;
He swore they would return with haste;
Whither they went I cannot tell—

Christabel

I thought I heard, some minutes past, 100
Sounds as of a castle bell.
Stretch forth thy hand " (thus ended she),
" And help a wretched maid to flee."

Then Christabel stretched forth her hand,
And comforted fair Geraldine: 105
" O well, bright dame! may you command
The service of Sir Leoline;
And gladly our stout chivalry,
Will he send forth and friends withal
To guide and guard you safe and free 110
Home to your noble father's hall."

She rose: and forth with steps they passed
That strove to be, and were not, fast.
Her gracious stars the lady blest,
And thus spake on sweet Christabel: 115
" All our household are at rest,
The hall as silent as the cell;
Sir Leoline is weak in health,
And may not well awakened be,
But we will move as if in stealth, 120
And I beseech your courtesy,
This night, to share your couch with me.'

They crossed the moat, and Christabel
Took the key that fitted well;
A little door she opened straight, 125
All in the middle of the gate;
The gate that was ironed within and without,
Where an army in battle array had marched out.
The lady sank, belike through pain,
And Christabel with might and main 130
Lifted her up, a weary weight,
Over the threshold of the gate:
Then the lady rose again,
And moved, as she were not in pain.

Christabel

So, free from danger, free from fear,
They crossed the court; right glad they were.
And Christabel devoutly cried
To the lady by her side,
"Praise we the Virgin all divine
Who hath rescued thee from thy distress!"
"Alas! alas!" said Geraldine,
"I cannot speak for weariness."
So, free from danger, free from fear,
They crossed the court; right glad they were.

Outside her kennel, the mastiff old
Lay fast asleep, in the moonshine cold.
The mastiff old did not awake,
Yet she an angry moan did make!
And what can ail the mastiff bitch?
Never till now she uttered yell
Beneath the eye of Christabel.
Perhaps it is the owlet's scritch:
For what can ail the mastiff bitch?

They passed the hall, that echoes still,
Pass as lightly as you will!
The brands were flat, the brands were dying,
Amid their own white ashes lying;
But when the lady passed, there came
A tongue of light, a fit of flame;
And Christabel saw the lady's eye,
And nothing else saw she thereby,
Save the boss of the shield of Sir Leoline tall,
Which hung in a murky old niche on the wall.
"O softly tread," said Christabel,
"My father seldom sleepeth well."

Sweet Christabel her feet doth bare,
And jealous of the listening air
They steal their way from stair to stair,

Christabel

Now in glimmer, and now in gloom,
And now they pass the Baron's room, 170
As still as death, with stifled breath!
And now have reached her chamber door;
And now doth Geraldine press down
The rushes of the chamber floor.

The moon shines dim in the open air, 175
And not a moonbeam enters here.
But they without its light can see
The chamber carved so curiously,
Carved with figures strange and sweet,
All made out of the carver's brain, 180
For a lady's chamber meet:
The lamp with twofold silver chain
Is fastened to an angel's feet.

The silver lamp burns dead and dim;
But Christabel the lamp will trim. 185
She trimmed the lamp, and made it bright,
And left it swinging to and fro,
While Geraldine, in wretched plight,
Sank down upon the floor below.

"O weary lady, Geraldine, 190
I pray you, drink this cordial wine!
It is a wine of virtuous powers;
My mother made it of wild flowers."

"And will your mother pity me,
Who am a maiden most forlorn?" 195
Christabel answered—"Woe is me!
She died the hour that I was born.
I have heard the grey-haired friar tell
How on her death-bed she did say,
That she should hear the castle-bell 200
Strike twelve upon my wedding-day.

Christabel

O mother dear! that thou wert here! "
" I would," said Geraldine, " she were! "

But soon with altered voice, said she—
" Off, wandering mother! Peak and pine! 205
I have power to bid thee flee."
Alas! What ails poor Geraldine?
Why stares she with unsettled eye?
Can she the bodiless dead espy?
And why with hollow voice cries she, 210
" Off, woman, off! this hour is mine—
Though thou her guardian spirit be,
Off, woman, off! 'tis given to me."

Then Christabel knelt by the lady's side,
And raised to heaven her eyes so blue— 215
" Alas! " said she, " this ghastly ride—
Dear lady! it hath wildered you! "
The lady wiped her moist cold brow,
And faintly said, " 'Tis over now! "

Again the wild-flower wine she drank: 220
Her fair large eyes 'gan glitter bright,
And from the floor whereon she sank,
The lofty lady stood upright:
She was most beautiful to see,
Like a lady of a far countrée. 225

And thus the lofty lady spake—
" All they who live in the upper sky,
Do love you, holy Christabel!
And you love them, and for their sake
And for the good which me befel, 230
Even I in my degree will try,
Fair maiden, to requite you well.
But now unrobe yourself; for I
Must pray, ere yet in bed I lie."

Christabel

Quoth Christabel, "So let it be!" 235
And as the lady bade, did she.
Her gentle limbs did she undress,
And lay down in her loveliness.

But through her brain of weal and woe
So many thoughts moved to and fro, 240
That vain it were her lids to close;
So half-way from the bed she rose,
And on her elbow did recline
To look at the lady Geraldine.

Beneath the lamp the lady bowed, 245
And slowly rolled her eyes around;
Then, drawing in her breath aloud,
Like one that shuddered, she unbound
The cincture from beneath her breast;
Her silken robe and inner vest 250
Dropt to her feet, and full in view,
Behold! her bosom and half her side—
A sight to dream of, not to tell!
O shield her! shield sweet Christabel!

Yet Geraldine nor speaks nor stirs; 255
Ah! what a stricken look was hers!
Deep from within she seems half-way
To lift some weight with sick assay,
And eyes the maid and seeks delay;
Then suddenly, as one defied, 260
Collects herself in scorn and pride,
And lay down by the Maiden's side!—
And in her arms the maid she took,
    Ah well-a-day!
And with low voice and doleful look 265
These words did say:
"In the touch of this bosom there worketh a spell,
Which is lord of thy utterance, Christabel!

Christabel

Thou knowest to-night, and wilt know to-morrow,
This mark of my shame, this seal of my sorrow; 270
    But vainly thou warrest,
      For this is alone in
    Thy power to declare,
      That in the dim forest
    Thou heard'st a low moaning, 275
And found'st a bright lady, surpassingly fair;
And didst bring her home with thee in love and in charity,
To shield her and shelter her from the damp air."

The Conclusion to Part the First

It was a lovely sight to see
The lady Christabel, when she 280
Was praying at the old oak tree.
    Amid the jaggéd shadows
    Of mossy leafless boughs,
    Kneeling in the moonlight,
    To make her gentle vows; 285
Her slender palms together prest,
Heaving sometimes on her breast;
Her face resigned to bliss or bale—
Her face, oh call it fair, not pale,
And both blue eyes more bright than clear, 290
Each about to have a tear.

With open eyes (ah woe is me!)
Asleep and dreaming fearfully,
Fearfully dreaming, yet, I wis,
Dreaming that alone, which is— 295
O sorrow and shame! Can this be she,
The lady, who knelt at the old oak tree?
And lo! the worker of these harms,
That holds the maiden in her arms,
Seems to slumber still and mild, 300
As a mother with her child.

Christabel

A star hath set, a star hath risen,
O Geraldine, since arms of thine
Have been the lovely lady's prison.
O Geraldine! one hour was thine—   305
Thou'st had thy will! By tairn and rill,
The night-birds all that hour were still.
But now they are jubilant anew,
From cliff and tower, tu-whoo! tu-whoo!
Tu-whoo! tu-whoo! from wood and fell!   310

And see the lady Christabel
Gathers herself from out her trance;
Her limbs relax, her countenance
Grows sad and soft; the smooth thin lids
Close o'er her eyes; and tears she sheds—   315
Large tears that leave the lashes bright!
And oft the while she seems to smile
As infants at a sudden light!

Yea, she doth smile, and she doth weep,
Like a youthful hermitess,   320
Beauteous in a wilderness,
Who, praying always, prays in sleep.
And, if she move unquietly,
Perchance, 'tis but the blood so free
Comes back and tingles in her feet.   325
No doubt, she hath a vision sweet.
What if her guardian spirit 'twere,
What if she knew her mother near?
But this she knows, in joys and woes,
That saints will aid if men will call: 330
For the blue sky bends over all!

Part the Second

"Each matin bell," the Baron saith,
"Knells us back to a world of death."
These words Sir Leoline first said,

Christabel

When he rose and found his lady dead: 335
These words Sir Leoline will say
Many a morn to his dying day!

And hence the custom and law began
That still at dawn the sacristan,
Who duly pulls the heavy bell, 340
Five and forty beads must tell
Between each stroke—a warning knell,
Which not a soul can choose but hear
From Bratha Head to Wyndermere.

Saith Bracy the bard, " So let it knell! 345
And let the drowsy sacristan
Still count as slowly as he can!
There is no lack of such, I ween,
As well fill up the space between.
In Langdale Pike and Witch's Lair 350
And Dungeon-ghyll so foully rent,
With ropes of rock and bells of air
Three sinful sextons' ghosts are pent,
Who all give back, one after t'other,
The death-note to their living brother; 355
And oft too, by the knell offended,
Just as their one! two! three is ended,
The devil mocks the doleful tale
With a merry peal from Borodale."

The air is still! through mist and cloud 360
That merry peal comes ringing loud;
And Geraldine shakes off her dread,
And rises lightly from the bed;
Puts on her silken vestments white,
And tricks her hair in lovely plight, 365
And nothing doubting of her spell
Awakens the lady Christabel.
" Sleep you, sweet lady Christabel?
I trust that you have rested well."

Christabel

And Christabel awoke and spied 370
The same who lay down by her side—
O rather say, the same whom she
Raised up beneath the old oak tree!
Nay, fairer yet! and yet more fair,
For she belike hath drunken deep 375
Of all the blessedness of sleep!
And while she spake, her looks, her air
Such gentle thankfulness declare,
That (so it seemed) her girded vests
Grew tight beneath her heaving breasts. 380
" Sure I have sinn'd! " said Christabel.
" Now heaven be praised, if all be well! "
And in low faltering tones, yet sweet,
Did she the lofty lady greet
With such perplexity of mind 385
As dreams too lively leave behind.

So quickly she rose, and quickly arrayed
Her maiden limbs, and having prayed
That He, who on the cross did groan,
Might wash away her sins unknown, 390
She forthwith led fair Geraldine
To meet her sire, Sir Leoline.

The lovely maid and the lady tall
Are pacing both into the hall,
And pacing on through page and groom, 395
Enter the Baron's presence-room.

The Baron rose, and while he prest
His gentle daughter to his breast,
With cheerful wonder in his eyes
The lady Geraldine espies, 400
And gave such welcome to the same,
As might beseem so bright a dame!

Christabel

But when he heard the lady's tale,
And when she told her father's name,
Why waxed Sir Leoline so pale, 405
Murmuring o'er the name again,
Lord Roland de Vaux of Tryermaine?

Alas! they had been friends in youth;
But whispering tongues can poison truth;
And constancy lives in realms above; 410
And life is thorny; and youth is vain;
And to be wroth with one we love
Doth work like madness in the brain.
And thus it chanced, as I divine,
With Roland and Sir Leoline. 415
Each spake words of high disdain
And insult to his heart's best brother:
They parted—ne'er to meet again!
But never either found another
To free the hollow heart from paining— 420
They stood aloof, the scars remaining,
Like cliffs which had been rent asunder;
A dreary sea now flows between;—
But neither heat, nor frost, nor thunder,
Shall wholly do away, I ween, 425
The marks of that which once hath been.

Sir Leoline, a moment's space,
Stood gazing on the damsel's face:
And the youthful lord of Tryermaine
Came back into his heart again. 430

O then the Baron forgot his age;
His noble heart swelled high with rage;
He swore by the wounds in Jesu's side
He would proclaim it far and wide,
With trump and solemn heraldry, 435
That they, who thus had wronged the dame,

Christabel

Were base as spotted infamy!
"And if they dare deny the same,
My herald shall appoint a week,
And let the recreant traitors seek 440
My tourney court—that there and then
I may dislodge their reptile souls
From the bodies and forms of men!"
He spake: his eye in lightning rolls!
For the lady was ruthlessly seized; and he kenned 445
In the beautiful lady the child of his friend!

And now the tears were on his face,
And fondly in his arms he took
Fair Geraldine, who met the embrace,
Prolonging it with joyous look. 450
Which when she viewed, a vision fell
Upon the soul of Christabel,
The vision of fear, the touch and pain!
She shrunk and shuddered, and saw again—
(Ah, woe is me! Was it for thee, 455
Thou gentle maid! such sights to see?)

Again she saw that bosom old,
Again she felt that bosom cold,
And drew in her breath with a hissing sound:
Whereat the Knight turned wildly round, 460
And nothing saw but his own sweet maid
With eyes upraised, as one that prayed.

The touch, the sight, had passed away,
And in its stead that vision blest,
Which comforted her after-rest 465
While in the lady's arm she lay,
Had put a rapture in her breast,
And on her lips and o'er her eyes
Spread smiles like light!
     With new surprise, 470

Christabel

"What ails then my beloved child?"
The Baron said—His daughter mild
Made answer, "All will yet be well!"
I ween, she had no power to tell
Aught else: so mighty was the spell. 475

Yet he who saw this Geraldine,
Had deemed her sure a thing divine:
Such sorrow with such grace she blended,
As if she feared she had offended
Sweet Christabel, that gentle maid! 480
And with such lowly tones she prayed
She might be sent without delay
Home to her father's mansion.
                              "Nay!
Nay, by my soul!" said Leoline. 485
"Ho, Bracy the bard, the charge be thine!
Go thou, with music sweet and loud,
And take two steeds with trappings proud,
And take the youth whom thou lov'st best
To bear thy harp, and learn thy song, 490
And clothe you both in solemn vest,
And over the mountains haste along,
Lest wandering folk, that are abroad,
Detain you on the valley road.

"And when he has crossed the Irthing flood, 495
My merry bard! he hastes, he hastes
Up Knorren Moor, through Halegarth Wood,
And reaches soon that castle good
Which stands and threatens Scotland's wastes.

"Bard Bracy! Bard Bracy! your horses are fleet, 500
Ye must ride up the hall, your music so sweet,
More loud than your horses' echoing feet!
And loud and loud to Lord Roland call,
Thy daughter is safe in Langdale hall!

Christabel

Thy beautiful daughter is safe and free— 505
Sir Leoline greets thee thus through me!
He bids thee come without delay
With all thy numerous array
And take thy lovely daughter home:
And he will meet thee on the way 510
With all his numerous array
White with their panting palfrey's foam:
And, by mine honour! I will say,
That I repent me of the day
When I spake words of fierce disdain 515
To Roland de Vaux of Tryermaine!—
—For since that evil hour hath flown,
Many a summer's sun hath shone;
Yet ne'er found I a friend again
Like Roland de Vaux of Tryermaine." 520

The lady fell, and clasped his knees,
Her face upraised, her eyes o'erflowing;
And Bracy replied, with faltering voice,
His gracious Hail on all bestowing!—
"Thy words, thou sire of Christabel, 525
Are sweeter than my harp can tell;
Yet might I gain a boon of thee,
This day my journey should not be,
So strange a dream hath come to me,
That I had vowed with music loud 530
To clear yon wood from thing unblest,
Warned by a vision in my rest!
For in my sleep I saw that dove,
That gentle bird, whom thou dost love,
And call'st by thy own daughter's name— 535
Sir Leoline! I saw the same
Fluttering, and uttering fearful moan,
Among the green herbs in the forest alone.
Which when I saw and when I heard,
I wonder'd what might ail the bird;

Christabel

For nothing near it could I see,
Save the grass and green herbs underneath the old tree.

" And in my dream methought I went
To search out what might there be found;
And what the sweet bird's trouble meant,   545
That thus lay fluttering on the ground.
I went and peered, and could descry
No cause for her distressful cry;
But yet for her dear lady's sake
I stooped, methought, the dove to take,   550
When lo! I saw a bright green snake
Coiled around its wings and neck.
Green as the herbs on which it couched,
Close by the dove's its head it crouched;
And with the dove it heaves and stirs,   555
Swelling its neck as she swelled hers!
I woke; it was the midnight hour,
The clock was echoing in the tower;
But though my slumber was gone by,
This dream it would not pass away—   560
It seems to live upon my eye!
And then I vowed this self-same day
With music strong and saintly song
To wander through the forest bare,
Lest aught unholy loiter there."   565

Thus Bracy said: the Baron, the while,
Half-listening heard him with a smile;
Then turned to Lady Geraldine,
His eyes made up of wonder and love;
And said in courtly accents fine,   570
" Sweet maid, Lord Roland's beauteous dove,
With arms more strong than harp or song,
Thy sire and I will crush the snake! "
He kissed her forehead as he spake,
And Geraldine in maiden wise   575

Christabel

Casting down her large bright eyes,
With blushing cheek and courtesy fine
She turned her from Sir Leoline;
Softly gathering up her train,
That o'er her right arm fell again; 580
And folded her arms across her chest,
And couched her head upon her breast,
And looked askance at Christabel—
Jesu, Maria, shield her well!

A snake's small eye blinks dull and shy; 585
And the lady's eyes they shrunk in her head,
Each shrunk up to a serpent's eye,
And with somewhat of malice and more of dread,
At Christabel she looked askance!—
One moment—and the sight was fled! 590
But Christabel in dizzy trance
Stumbling on the unsteady ground
Shuddered aloud, with a hissing sound;
And Geraldine again turned round,
And like a thing that sought relief, 595
Full of wonder and full of grief,
She rolled her large bright eyes divine
Wildly on Sir Leoline.

The maid, alas! her thoughts are gone,
She nothing sees—no sight but one! 600
The maid, devoid of guile and sin,
I know not how, in fearful wise,
So deeply had she drunken in
That look, those shrunken serpent eyes,
That all her features were resigned 605
To this sole image in her mind:
And passively did imitate
That look of dull and treacherous hate!
And thus she stood, in dizzy trance,
Still picturing that look askance 610

Christabel

With forced unconscious sympathy
Full before her father's view—
As far as such a look could be
In eyes so innocent and blue.

And when the trance was o'er, the maid   615
Paused awhile, and inly prayed:
Then falling at the Baron's feet,
" By my mother's soul do I entreat
That thou this woman send away! "
She said: and more she could not say;   620
For what she knew she could not tell,
O'er-mastered by the mighty spell.

Why is thy cheek so wan and wild,
Sir Leoline? Thy only child
Lies at thy feet, thy joy, thy pride,   625
So fair, so innocent, so mild;
The same, for whom thy lady died!
O by the pangs of her dear mother
Think thou no evil of thy child!
For her, and thee, and for no other,   630
She prayed the moment ere she died:
Prayed that the babe for whom she died,
Might prove her dear lord's joy and pride!
    That prayer her deadly pangs beguiled,
      Sir Leoline!   635
    And wouldst thou wrong thy only child,
      Her child and thine?

Within the Baron's heart and brain
If thoughts, like these, had any share,
They only swelled his rage and pain,   640
And did but work confusion there.
His heart was cleft with pain and rage,
His cheeks they quivered, his eyes were wild,
Dishonoured thus in his old age;

Christabel

Dishonoured by his only child, 645
And all his hospitality
To the wronged daughter of his friend
By more than woman's jealousy
Brought thus to a disgraceful end—
He rolled his eye with stern regard 650
Upon the gentle minstrel bard,
And said in tones abrupt, austere—
" Why, Bracy, dost thou loiter here?
I bade thee hence! " The bard obeyed;
And turning from his own sweet maid, 655
The agéd knight, Sir Leoline,
Led forth the lady Geraldine!

THE CONCLUSION TO PART THE SECOND

A little child, a limber elf,
Singing, dancing to itself,
A fairy thing with red round cheeks, 660
That always finds and never seeks,
Makes such a vision to the sight
As fills a father's eyes with light;
And pleasures flow in so thick and fast
Upon his heart, that he at last 665
Must needs express his love's excess
With words of unmeant bitterness.
Perhaps 'tis pretty to force together
Thoughts so all unlike each other;
To mutter and mock a broken charm, 670
To dally with wrong that does no harm.
Perhaps 'tis tender too and pretty
At each wild word to feel within
A sweet recoil of love and pity.
And what, if in a world of sin 675
(O sorrow and shame should this be true!)
Such giddiness of heart and brain
Comes seldom save from rage and pain,
So talks as it's most used to do.

KUBLA KHAN

In Xanadu did Kubla Khan
A stately pleasure-dome decree:
Where Alph, the sacred river, ran,
Through caverns measureless to man
    Down to a sunless sea. 5
So twice five miles of fertile ground
With walls and towers were girdled round:
And there were gardens bright with sinuous rills,
Where blossomed many an incense-bearing tree;
And here were forests ancient as the hills, 10
Enfolding sunny spots of greenery.

But oh! that deep romantic chasm which slanted
Down the green hill athwart a cedarn cover!
A savage place! as holy and enchanted
As e'er beneath a waning moon was haunted 15
By woman wailing for her demon-lover!
And from this chasm, with ceaseless turmoil seething,
As if this earth in fast thick pants were breathing,
A mighty fountain momently was forced:
Amid whose swift half-intermitted burst 20
Huge fragments vaulted like rebounding hail,
Or chaffy grain beneath the thresher's flail:
And 'mid these dancing rocks at once and ever
It flung up momently the sacred river.
Five miles meandering with a mazy motion 25
Through wood and dale the sacred river ran,
Then reached the caverns measureless to man,
And sank in tumult to a lifeless ocean:
And 'mid this tumult Kubla heard from far
Ancestral voices prophesying war! 30
    The shadow of the dome of pleasure
    Floated midway on the waves;
    Where was heard the mingled measure
    From the fountain and the caves.

Kubla Khan

It was a miracle of rare device, 35
A sunny pleasure-dome with caves of ice!

    A damsel with a dulcimer
    In a vision once I saw:
    It was an Abyssinian maid,
    And on her dulcimer she played, 40
    Singing of Mount Abora.
    Could I revive within me
    Her symphony and song,
    To such deep delight 'twould win me,
That with music loud and long 45
I would build that dome in air,
That sunny dome! those caves of ice!
And all who heard should see them there,
And all should cry, Beware! Beware!
His flashing eyes, his floating hair! 50
Weave a circle round him thrice,
And close your eyes with holy dread,
For he on honey-dew hath fed,
And drunk the milk of Paradise.

FANCY IN NUBIBUS
Or The Poet in The Clouds

O! It is pleasant with a heart at ease,
   Just after sunset, or by moonlight skies,
To make the shifting clouds be what you please,
   Or let the easily persuaded eyes
Own each quaint likeness issuing from the mould
   Of a friend's fancy; or with head bent low
And cheek aslant see rivers flow of gold
   'Twixt crimson banks; and then, a traveller, go
From mount to mount through Cloudland, gorgeous land!
   Or list'ning to the tide, with closéd sight,
Be that blind bard, who on the Chian strand
   By those deep sounds possessed with inward light
Beheld the Iliad and Odyssey
   Rise to the swelling of the voiceful sea.

TIME, REAL AND IMAGINARY
An Allegory

On the wide level of a mountain's head,
(I knew not where, but 'twas some faery place)
Their pinions, ostrich-like, for sails outspread,
Two lovely children run an endless race,
    A sister and a brother!
    This far outstript the other;
Yet ever runs she with reverted face,
And looks and listens for the boy behind:
    For he, alas! is blind!
O'er rough and smooth with even step he passed,
And knows not whether he be first or last.

THE DEVIL'S THOUGHTS

From his brimstone bed at break of day
A walking the Devil is gone,
To visit his little snug farm of the earth
And see how his stock went on.

Over the hill and over the dale,
And he went over the plain,
And backward and forward he swished his long tail
As a gentleman swishes his cane.

And how then was the Devil drest?
Oh! he was in his Sunday's best:
His jacket was red and his breeches were blue.
And there was a hole where his tail came through.
*   *   *   *   *   *

He saw a cottage with a double coach-house,
  A cottage of gentility!
And the Devil did grin for his darling sin
  Is pride that apes humility.
*   *   *   *   *   *

As he went through Cold-Bath Fields he saw
  A solitary cell,
And the Devil was pleased, for it gave him a hint
  For improving his prisons in Hell.
*   *   *   *   *   *

General ——— burning face
  He saw with consternation,
And back to Hell his way did he take,
For the Devil thought by a slight mistake
  It was a general conflagration.

FRANCE: AN ODE

I

Ye Clouds! that far above me float and pause,
   Whose pathless march no mortal may control!
   Ye Ocean-Waves! that, wheresoe'er ye roll,
Yield homage only to eternal laws!
Ye woods! that listen to the night-birds singing,
   Midway the smooth and perilous slope reclined,
Save when your own imperious branches swinging,
   Have made a solemn music of the wind!
Where, like a man beloved of God,
Through glooms which never woodman trod,
   How oft, pursuing fancies holy,
My moonlight way o'er flowering weeds I wound,
   Inspired, beyond the guess of folly,
By each rude shape and wild unconquerable sound!
O ye loud Waves! and O ye Forests high!
   And O ye clouds that far above me soared!
Thou rising Sun, thou blue rejoicing Sky!
Yea, every thing that is and will be free!
Bear witness for me, wheresoe'er ye be,
   With what deep worship I have still adored
The spirit of divinest Liberty.

II

When France in wrath her giant-limbs upreared,
   And with that oath, which smote air, earth, and sea,
   Stamped her strong foot and said she would be free,
Bear witness for me, how I hoped and feared!
With what a joy my lofty gratulation
   Unawed I sang, amid a slavish band:
And when to whelm the disenchanted nation,

France

Like fiends embattled by a wizard's wand,
Then Monarchs marched in evil day,
And Britain joined the dire array;
Though dear her shores and circling ocean,
  Though many friendships, many youthful loves,
Had swoln the patriot emotion,
  And flung a magic light o'er all her hills and groves;
Yet still my voice, unaltered, sang defeat,
  To all that braved the tyrant-quelling lance,
And shame too long delayed and vain retreat!
For ne'er, O Liberty! with partial aim
I dimmed thy light or damped thy holy flame;
  But blessed the pæans of delivered France,
And hung my head and wept at Britain's name.

III

" And what," I said, " though Blasphemy's loud scream
  With that sweet music of deliverance strove!
  Though all the fierce and drunken passions wove
A dance more wild than e'er was maniac's dream!
  Ye storms, that round the dawning east assembled,
The Sun was rising, though he hid his light!
  And when, to soothe my soul, that hoped and trembled,
The dissonance ceased, and all seemed calm and bright;
When France her front deep-scarr'd and gory
Concealed with clustering wreaths of glory;
When, insupportably advancing,
  Her arm made mockery of the warrior's tramp;
While timid looks of fury glancing,
  Domestic treason, crushed beneath her fatal stamp,
Writhed like a wounded dragon in his gore;
  Then I reproached my fears that would not flee;
" And soon," I said, " shall Wisdom teach her lore
In the low huts of them that toil and groan!
And, conquering by her happiness alone,
  Shall France compel the nations to be free,
Till Love and Joy look round, and call the Earth their own."

France

IV

Forgive me, Freedom! O forgive those dreams!
   I hear thy voice, I hear thy loud lament,
   From Bleak Helvetia's icy cavern sent—
I hear thy groans upon her blood-stained streams!
   Heroes, that for your peaceful country perished,
And ye that, fleeing, spot your mountain-snows
   With bleeding wounds; forgive me, that I cherished
One thought that ever blessed your cruel foes!
    To scatter rage, and traitorous guilt,
    Where Peace her jealous home had built;
     A patriot-race to disinherit
Of all that made their stormy wilds so dear;
     And with inexpiable spirit
To taint the bloodless freedom of the mountaineer—
O France, that mockest Heaven, adulterous, blind,
   And patriot only in pernicious toils,
Are these thy boasts, Champion of humankind?
To mix with Kings in the low lust of sway,
Yell in the hunt, and share the murderous prey;
To insult the shrine of Liberty with spoils
   From freemen torn; to tempt and to betray?

V

   The Sensual and the Dark rebel in vain,
Slaves by their own compulsion! In mad game
They burst their manacles and wear the name
   Of Freedom, graven on a heavier chain!
   O Liberty! with profitless endeavor
Have I pursued thee, many a weary hour;
   But thou nor swell'st the victor's strain, nor ever
Didst breathe thy soul in forms of human power,
    Alike from all, howe'er they praise thee
    (Nor prayer, nor boastful name delays thee),
    Alike from Priestcraft's harpy minions,
And factious Blasphemy's obscener slaves,

France

    Thou speedest on thy subtle pinions,
The guide of homeless winds, and playmate of the waves!
And there I felt thee!—on that sea-cliff's verge,
    Whose pines, scarce travelled by the breeze above,
Had made one murmur with the distant surge!
Yes, while I stood and gazed, my temples bare,
And shot my being through earth, sea, and air,
    Possessing all things with intensest love,
O Liberty! my spirit felt thee there.

LOVE

All thoughts, all passions, all delights,
    Whatever stirs this mortal frame,
All are but ministers of Love,
    And feed his sacred flame.

Oft in my waking dreams do I
    Live o'er again that happy hour,
When midway on the mount I lay,
    Beside the ruined tower.

The moonshine, stealing o'er the scene,
    Had blended with the lights of eve;
And she was there, my hope, my joy,
    My own dear Genevieve!

She leaned against the armèd man,
    The statue of the armèd knight;
She stood and listened to my lay,
    Amid the lingering light.

Few sorrows hath she of her own,
    My hope! my joy! my Genevieve!
She loves me best, whene'er I sing
    The songs that make her grieve.

I played a soft and doleful air,
    I sang an old and moving story—
And old rude song, that suited well
    That ruin wild and hoary.

Love

She listened with a flitting blush,
    With downcast eyes and modest grace;
For well she knew, I could not choose
    But gaze upon her face.

I told her of the Knight that wore
    Upon his shield a burning brand;
And that for ten long years he wooed
    The Lady of the Land.

I told her how he pined: and ah!
    The deep, the low, the pleading tone
With which I sang another's love,
    Interpreted my own.

She listened with a flitting blush,
    With downcast eyes, and modest grace;
And she forgave me, that I gazed
    Too fondly on her face!

But when I told the cruel scorn
    That crazed that bold and lovely Knight,
And that he crossed the mountain-woods,
    Nor rested day nor night;

That sometimes from the savage den,
    And sometimes from the darksome shade,
And sometimes starting up at once
    In green and sunny glade,—

There came and looked him in the face
    An angel beautiful and bright:
And that he knew it was a Fiend
    This miserable Knight!

And that, unknowing what he did,
    He leaped amid a murderous band,
And saved from outrage worse than death
    The Lady of the Land;—

Love

And how she wept, and clasped her knees;
  And how she tended him in vain—
And ever strove to expiate
  The scorn that crazed his brain;—

And that she nursed him in a cave;
  And how his madness went away,
When on the yellow forest leaves
  A dying man he lay;—

His dying words—but when I reached
  That tenderest strain of all the ditty,
My faltering voice and pausing harp
  Disturbed her soul with pity!

All impulses of soul and sense
  Had thrilled my guileless Genevieve;
The music and the doleful tale,
  The rich and balmy eve;

And hopes, and fears that kindle hope,
  An undistinguishable throng,
And gentle wishes long subdued,
  Subdued and cherished long!

She wept with pity and delight,
  She blushed with love and virgin shame;
And like the murmur of a dream
  I heard her breathe my name.

Her bosom heaved—she stepped aside,
  As conscious of my look she stept—
Then suddenly, with timorous eye,
  She fled to me and wept.

She half enclosed me with her arms;
  She pressed me with a meek embrace;
And bending back her head, looked up,
  And gazed upon my face.

Love

'Twas partly love, and partly fear,
    And partly 'twas a bashful art,
That I might rather feel, than see,
    The swelling of her heart.

I calmed her fears, and she was calm,
    And told her love with virgin pride;
And so I won my Genevieve,
    My bright and beauteous Bride.

ANSWER TO A CHILD'S QUESTION

Do you ask what the birds say? The sparrow, the dove,
The linnet, and thrush, say, " I love and I love! "
In the winter they're silent—the wind is so strong.
What it says I don't know, but it sings a loud song.
But green leaves, and blossoms, and sunny warm weather,
And singing, and loving—all come back together.
But the lark is so brimful of gladness and love,
The green fields below him, the blue sky above,
That he sings and he sings; and forever sings he—
" I love my Love, and my Love loves me! "

YOUTH AND AGE

Verse, a breeze mid blossoms straying,
Where Hope clung feeding, like a bee—
Both were mine! Life went a-maying
    With Nature, Hope, and Poesy,
        When I was young!

When I was young?—Ah, woeful When!
Ah! for the change 'twixt Now and Then!
This breathing house not built with hands,
This body that does me grievous wrong,
O'er aery cliffs and glittering sands,
How lightly then it flashed along:—
Like those trim skiffs, unknown of yore,
On winding lakes and rivers wide,
That ask no air of sail or oar,
That fear no spite of wind or tide!
Naught cared this body for wind or weather
When Youth and I lived in't together.

Flowers are lovely; Love is flower-like;
Friendship is a sheltering tree;
O! the joys, that came down shower-like,
Of Friendship, Love, and Liberty,
        Ere I was old!

Ere I was old—Ah, woeful Ere
Which tells me, Youth's no longer here!
O Youth! for years so many and sweet,
'Tis known, that thou and I were one,
I'll think it but a fond conceit—
It cannot be that thou art gone!
The vesper-bell hath not yet tolled:—

Youth and Age

And thou wert aye a masker bold!
What strange disguise hast now put on,
To make believe, that thou art gone?
I see these locks in silvery slips,
This drooping gait, this altered size:
But Springtide blossoms on thy lips,
And tears take sunshine from thine eyes!
Life is but thought: so think I will
That Youth and I are house-mates still.

Dew-drops are the gems of morning,
But the tears of mournful eve!
Where no hope is, life's a warning
That only serves to make us grieve,
                When we are old:

That only serves to make us grieve
With oft and tedious taking-leave,
Like some poor nigh-related guest,
That may not rudely be dismist;
Yet hath outstayed his welcome while,
And tells the jest without the smile.

LESSON FOR A BOY

Trochee | trips from | long to | short;
From long | to long | in sol|emn sort
Slow Spon|dee stalks; | strong foot, yet | ill able
Ever to | come up with | Dactyl tri|syllable;
Iam|bics march | from short | to long;
With a leap | and a bound | the swift An|apæsts throng;
One sylla|ble long, with | a short at | each side,
Amphibra|chys hastes with | a stately | stride;
First and last | being long, | middle short, | Amphimac|er
Strikes his thun|dering hoofs | like a proud | high-bred rac|er.

THE HOMERIC HEXAMETER

Strongly it | bears us a|long in | swelling and | limitless billows—
Nothing be|fore and | nothing be|hind but the | sky and the | ocean.

HEXAMETER AND PENTAMETER

In the hex|ameter | rises the | fountain's | silvery | column,
In the pent|ameter | aye | falling in | melody | back.

LETTER TO WILLIAM AND DOROTHY WORDSWORTH

William, my teacher, my friend! dear William and dear
    Dorothea!
Smooth out the folds of my letter, and place it on desk or
    on table;
Place it on table or desk; and your right hands loosely
    half-closing,
Gently sustain them in air, and extending the digit didactic,
Rest it a moment on each of the forks of the five-forkéd
    left hand,
Twice on the breadth of the thumb, and once on the tip of
    each finger,
Read with a nod of the head in a humoring recitativo;
And, as I live, you will see my hexameters hopping be-
    fore you.
This is a galloping measure; a hop, and a trot, and a gallop!

All my hexameters fly, like stags pursued by the stag-hounds,
Breathless and panting, and ready to drop, yet flying still
    onwards,
I would full fain pull in my hard-mouthed runaway hunter;
But our English Spondeans are clumsy yet impotent curb-
    reins;
And so to make him go slowly, no way left have I but to
    lame him.

William, my head and my heart! dear Poet that feelest
    and thinkest!
Dorothy, eager of soul, my most affectionate sister!
Many a mile, O! many a wearisome mile are ye distant,
Long, long comfortless roads, with no one eye that doth
    know us.
O! it is all too far to send you mockeries idle:

Letter

Yea, and I feel it not right! But O! my friends, my beloved!
Feverish and wakeful I lie—I am weary of feeling and
    thinking.
Every thought is worn down, I am weary yet cannot be
    vacant.

    *   *   *   *   *

. . . . my eyes are a burthen,
Now unwillingly closed, now open and aching with darkness.
O! what a life is the eye! what a fine and inscrutable essence!
Him that is utterly blind, nor glimpses the fire that warms
    him;
Him that never beheld the swelling breast of his mother·
Him that smiled in his gladness as babe that smiles in
    its slumber;
Even for him it exists, it stirs and moves in its prison;
Lives with a separate life, and ' Is it a Spirit? ' he murmurs,
' Sure it has thoughts of its own, and to see is only a
    language.'

    *   *   *   *   *

William my head and my heart! dear William and dear
    Dorothea!
You have all in each other; but I am lonely, and want you!

THE KNIGHT'S TOMB

Where is the grave of Sir Arthur O'Kellyn?
Where may the grave of that good man be?—
By the side of a spring, on the breast of Helvellyn,
Under the twigs of a young birch tree!
The oak that in summer was sweet to hear,
And rustled its leaves in the fall of the year,
And whistled and roar'd in the winter alone,
Is gone—and the birch in its stead is grown.
The Knight's bones are dust,
And his good sword rust;—
His soul is with the saints, I trust.

EPITAPH

Stop, Christian passer-by! Stop, child of God,
And read with gentle breast. Beneath this sod
A poet lies, or that which once seem'd he.
O, lift one thought in prayer for S. T. C.;
That he who many a year with toil of breath
Found death in life, may here find life in death!
Mercy for praise—to be forgiven for fame
He ask'd, and hoped, through Christ.
    Do thou the same!

NOTES ON THE ANCIENT MARINER

IN the first edition an "Argument" was prefixed to the poem: "How a Ship having passed the Line was driven by storms to the cold Country towards the South Pole; and how from thence she made her course to the tropical Latitude of the great Pacific Ocean; and of the strange things that befell; and in what manner the Ancyent Marinere came back to his own Country." This was omitted, and the marginal glosses were added and the motto from Burnet, when the poem appeared in *Sibylline Leaves*, 1817.

1. As in the traditional ballads, the poet begins without preliminaries, and the speeches of the characters are sometimes not assigned, but may be inferred from the context. The whole introduction moves with swiftness and brevity. In the descriptions, the attention is riveted by the exactness, though fewness of the details, *e.g.*, one of *three* is stopped. The Mariner is not fully described, but there is sufficient visual suggestion to make one see the whole figure.

8. The omission of the subject of the verb adds to the effect of haste.

Between the second and fourth stanzas these verses occurred, in the first edition:

> But still he holds the wedding-guest—
> There was a Ship, quoth he—
> 'Nay, if thou'st got a laughsome tale,
> Marinere! come with me.'
>
> He holds him with his skinny hand,
> Quoth he, there was a Ship—
> 'Now get thee hence, thou grey-beard Loon!
> Or my staff shall make thee skip.'

9. The Mariner seems not to hear the protest. Soon he has the Wedding Guest so fascinated that he cannot go.

11. **loon.** Suggested perhaps by the "cream-faced loon" of *Macbeth*, V, iii, 11.

12. **Eftsoons.** Straightway.

20. **Mariner.** Here the word takes a slight accent on the last syllable—the "wrenched" or "forced" accent of the old ballads.

21. Already the voyage has begun—the ship is under way.

22. **drop.** Sailor's term.

23. **kirk.** Church. Scottish form. Used in the ballads.

Notes on the Ancient Mariner

25. **sun . . . left.** They are sailing southward.
Line. Old word for the Equator.

32. **bassoon.** Coleridge's biographer and editor, J. Dykes Campbell, notes that according to the suggestion of Mrs. Sandford, author of *Thomas Poole and His Friends,* Coleridge got the idea of a bassoon from the fact that his friend Poole introduced one into the church choir, during his residence at Nether Stowey.

34. **Red as a rose.** An old simile. Compare Burns's " My love is like a red, red rose."

35. **Nodding.** Because of the effect of the music.

40. These verses follow, in the first edition, between lines 40 and 45:

> Listen, Stranger! Storm and Wind,
> A Wind and Tempest Strong!
> For days and weeks it play'd us freaks—
> Like chaff we drove along.
>
> Listen, Stranger! Mist and Snow,
> And it grew wondrous cauld;
> And Ice mast-high came floating by
> As green as Emerauld.

In the 1800 edition of the *Lyrical Ballads* the following stanza appeared between lines 40 and 51.

> But now the Northwind came more fierce,
> There came a Tempest strong!
> And Southward still for days and weeks
> Like Chaff we drove along.

The present stanzas (ll. 41-50) were added in 1817.

41. **Storm-blast.** Coleridge liked such pleonastic compounds. Compare *fog-smoke,* l. 77, and *skiff-boat,* l. 523. The personification should be noted. One critic points out that it is to prepare the way for a world in which the weather and the birds and sea-monsters are almost as human as man. The violence of the images for the rest of the Part, while the ship passes through the ice-fields, is striking. They are of yelling, driving, roaring, cracking, growling, howling, splitting.

50. **aye.** Ever. Pronounced, in this meaning, not like *aye,* 'yes,' but like the indefinite article.

55. **clifts.** Snow-filled clefts of ice. The word sounds like a blend of *cliffs* and *clefts.* Used by Spenser, *Faerie Queen,* III, IV, vii.

56. **sheen.** Light like that of a snow-storm.

57. **ken.** Scottish for *know.*

61. "Ice mast-high (l. 53), and "It cracked and growl'd,

Notes on the Ancient Mariner

etc., may have been suggested by certain passages in Captain James's *Strange and Dangerous Voyage*, etc., namely: "We had Ice not farre off about us, and some pieces as high as our Top-mast head," p. 7; "It [the ice] made a hollow and hideous noyse, like an over-fall of water," p. 8; "The Ice began to breake with a most terrible thundering noyse," p. 12. Thomas Hutchinson points out that Captain James's *Epitaph on Companions left behind in the Northern Seas* was included by Wordsworth in the album of poems and extracts presented by him to Lady Mary Lowther in 1819.

62. **swound.** Swoon. Used in Percy's ballad, *Sir Cauline*. The word gives a remote and ghostly effect to the noises in the preceding line.

63. **albatross.** Hailed by the crew because it was a bird of good omen. In Shelvock's *Voyage Round the World by the Way of the Great South Sea*, he calls albatrosses "the largest sort of sea-fowls, some of them extending their wings twelve or thirteen foot."

64. **Thorough.** Old form for *through*.

67. **eat.** Here the effect is archaic. The form *eat* as a past participle is now in vulgar usage only.

69. **thunder-fit.** With a sound like thunder.

76. **vespers nine.** Nine evenings. Notice the partiality for odd numbers.

77. **Whiles.** Old form of *while*.
    fog-smoke. See note on l. 41.

79–81. These lines suggest the change which comes over the expression of the Mariner, as he remembers his deed.

81. **cross-bow.** A mediæval weapon formed of a bow set cross-wise on a stock. It discharged bolts, arrows, stones, etc.

The shooting of the bird, with which the Part ends, forms a climax and turning point in the narrative.

II. The ballad effect of iteration is much used along here. The first stanza of this part is varied from the VII of the preceding, while the next echoes XVIII. Stanzas XXIII and XXIV are swelled to six lines, with the duplication of a line in each, and both show interior rhymes.

83. **right.** They have now turned northward.

91. **a hellish thing.** Peril at sea has often been associated in legend with the evil-doing of some one on shipboard.

92. **'em.** Archaic for *them*.

98. **uprist.** Uprose. Found in Chaucer and Spenser.

104. **The furrow followed.** Coleridge changed "followed" to "streamed off," in *Sibylline Leaves*, 1817, with this note: "But I had not been long on board a ship when I perceived that this

Notes on the Ancient Mariner

was the image seen by a spectator from the shore, or from another vessel. From the ship itself the wake appears like a brook flowing off from the shore." He later restored the original reading. In so doing he did well. As it now stands, the whole stanza is one of the finest examples in English poetry of onomatopœia. The *f*'s in the *furrow followed free* reproduce the sound made by the prow as it cuts through successive waves, the *s*'s in the last two lines the sound of the water as it flows away from the ship.

The images called up along here are of flying, bursting, etc. There is ebbing of sound and motion, from the violence of the preceding scenes, until the absolute contrast of the calm is reached.

105. Notice the effective use of the simple word *burst*.

107. The motion is perceptibly slowed at this point.

111. **All.** Having little more than intensive force. Used in a poetic or archaic way, as in Spenser.

116. **stuck.** Another simple word, used effectively.

125. **with legs.** Notice the added intensity given by this detail to the visual suggestion of the "crawling things."

127. **rout.** Moving throng, or disorderly group.

128. **death-fires.** Phosphorescent lights, sometimes called St. Elmo's lights. Contrast the pictures of sunrise, of the hot and copper sky, of the slimy things on the water, and of the dance of the death-fires, while the water burns as with "witches' oils"— a passage of vivid color—with the green and white of the ice-field scenes in Part I.

132. **Josephus,** the first of the learned authorities mentioned in the gloss, was a Jewish historian of the first century.

Michael Psellus taught philosophy in the eleventh century in Constantinople. He wrote a treatise on Demonology.

139. **well-a-day.** Alas. Archaic.

This part also ends with a reference to the albatross. The hanging about the Mariner's neck of the albatross, in place of a crucifix, is his first punishment.

III. There are more interweaving repetitions, in the ballad manner, in this part.

143. The weariness of the crew is reflected in the lengthening out of the stanza.

These lines originally followed, in the first edition:

>   I saw a something in the sky
>   No bigger than my fist;
>   At first it seem'd a little speck, etc.

In the next edition (1800) they read:—

>   So past a weary time, each throat
>   Was parch'd and glaz'd each eye,
>   When looking westward, etc.

Notes on the Ancient Mariner

The stanza appeared in its present form in 1817.

148. **something.** This rivets the attention and excites curiosity.

152. **wist.** Knew. Archaic.

155–56. Strongly suggestive, visually, of the waywardness of the motion.

157. Originally:

> With throat unslack'd, with black lips bak'd
>   Ne could we laugh, ne wail:
> Then while thro' drouth all dumb they stood
> I bit my arm and suck'd the blood
>   And cry'd, A sail! a sail!

158. **nor . . . nor,** for *neither . . . nor* is archaic and poetic.

164. **Gramercy.** Mediæval ejaculation. From the French expression meaning thanks.

for joy did grin. Their mouths were distorted by thirst. Compare Coleridge's notes, *Biographia Literaria*, 1847, ii, 343, and *Table Talk,* May 31, 1830. He says: "Brookes, Berdmore, and myself, at the imminent hazard of our lives, scaled the very summit of Penmaenmaur. It was a most dreadful expedition." "We were nearly dead with thirst, and could not speak from constriction till we found a little puddle under a stone. Berdmore said to me: 'You grinned like an idiot!' He had done the same."

165–66. A suggestive comparison, visually and orally.

167–170. These lines read originally:—

> She doth not tack from side to side—
>   Hither to work us weal
> Withouten wind, withouten tide
>   She steddies with upright keel.

These stanzas were originally present between lines 184–190:

> Are those *her* naked ribs, which fleck'd
>   The sun that did behind them peer?
> And are those two all, all the crew,
>   That woman and her fleshless Pheere?

> *His* bones were black with many a crack,
>   All black and bare, I ween:
> Jet-black and bare, save where with rust
> Of mouldy damps and charnel crust
>   They're patch'd with purple and green.

Various other experimental stanzas were tried by the poet before

Notes on the Ancient Mariner

the present form of the passage was adopted. The next stanza also was changed considerably, with resultant improvement in simplicity and compactness.

170. **steadies.** The variation of the rhythm, changing from iambic to anapæstic midway in the line, is suggestive of the change in the ship's movement.

184. **gossameres.** Fine cobwebs.

190. The description of the strange motion of the ship is interrupted by a color description of Life-in-Death. The figure of Death is too familiar to need description. The suggestion of red lips, yellow hair, joined to skin "white as leprosy," produces a dread effect.

198. **thrice.** An odd number again.

202. The disappearance of the skeleton ship against the sun is as rapid as its appearance. One critic has suggested that the Mariner might not really have seen the spectral bark—that it was but the hallucination of a fever.

199. Lines 199-218 read originally:

> A gust of wind sterte up behind
> And whistled thro' his bones;
> Thro' the holes of his eyes and the hole of his mouth
> Half-whistles and half-groans.
>
> With never a whisper in the Sea
> Off darts the Spectre-ship,
> While clombe above the Eastern bar
> The horned Moon, with one bright Star
> Almost atween the tips.
>
> One after one by the horned Moon
> (Listen, O stranger! to me)
> Each turn'd his face with a ghastly pang
> And curs'd me with his ee.

Coleridge tried and discarded many other stanzas and lines in this part of the poem. The passage describing the skeleton ship and its occupants was that which gave him the greatest trouble.

203. **sideways.** Not straight at. They were frightened. This nine-line stanza, the longest in the poem, draws out the fear and dread of the sailors, in the night. Note the contrast, after the rapid motion of the spectre ship.

209. **clomb.** Old form of *climbed*.

211. **nether.** No star is ever in this position. Coleridge v thinking of the sailor's superstition that a star dogging the ɪ presages bad luck.

Notes on the Ancient Mariner

218. thump . . . lump. More commonplace words, used tellingly by the poet. They help to make real the sudden death of the Mariner's fellow sailors, with which the part ends.

223. The last line of the part takes us back to the death of the albatross.

IV. Subtle repetition is continued in this part, and there is occasional alliteration. Part IV. is largely subjective; it is devoted almost wholly to the feelings of the Ancient Mariner. All sound effects are hushed. The part is gentler than the preceding; there is little actual motion, but rather pause from it. Another passage of contrasted color occurs in the description of the water-snakes.

226. A note by Coleridge, first printed in *Sibylline Leaves*, 1817, reads: "For the last two lines of this stanza I am indebted to Mr. Wordsworth. It was on a delightful walk from Nether Stowey to Dulverton, with him and his sister, in the autumn of 1797, that this poem was planned, and in part composed."

227. ribbed. Suggestive of the effect left by receding waves on the sea sand.

232. Alone, etc. Note the echoic quality of the line. The sound reflects the meaning and the mood. Lines 233-34 read originally:

> Alone on the wide wide sea;
> And Christ would take no pity on, etc.

236 ff. Note the state of mind registered here.

245-47. gusht . . . dust. Imperfect rhyme.

248. Another lengthened stanza. The anapæsts of l. 250, have the effect of retarding. They emphasize the Mariner's weariness, lethargy, and loneliness. More often Coleridge uses this foot to produce the effect of acceleration.

254. reek. Smell. Used for alliteration. The older form of the line was:

> Ne rot ne reek did they:

257. Another change in the stanzaic length and movement.

261. seven. Odd number again.

263. The turning point in the story is near, and it is accompanied by marked variation in the meter. The Mariner looks up at the moon and the stars; when he looks down again and sees the water-snakes it is in a new way.

265. **Softly**, etc. A simple but telling line.

268. Improved from the original line, with its Chaucerian past participle:

> Like morning frosts y-spread.

Notes on the Ancient Mariner

271. Another color passage begins, with slightly changed stanza and rhyme effect.

275. **elfish.** *Elfin* and *elvish* are related words with similar meaning.

284. The turning point, or climax, in the narrative. To the Mariner, who could kill the albatross, even the water snakes have become beautiful; love gushes from his heart, because they are living things. With his emancipation of spirit the curse begins to fail; the albatross falls from his neck like the pack from Christian's back in *The Pilgrim's Progress*. A passage in *The Travels of Sir Richard Hawkins* may have suggested the colored watersnake passage. See *The Nation*, April 2, 1914, p. 360.

286. **Sure.** Archaic, in this initial adverbial use. Not to be confused with the modern slang usage, as in " I sure do," etc.

V. This part opens quietly. The Mariner has been forgiven and his regeneration begins. Soon comes a new series of violent and abnormal motions. The images are of roaring air, upper winds, wan stars dancing, wind, hail, lightning. The dead men stir. A musical interval brings relief, and restful sweet sounds are heard, as morning dawns.

297. **silly.** Empty, vain. The word first meant blessed, like the German *selig;* in its next stages it meant innocent, happy, simple, foolish.

303. **sure.** See note on l. 286.

drunken. Old past participle.

308. **blessèd ghost**, *i.e.*, spirit, as in *Holy Ghost*. An older meaning of the word.

312. **sere.** Like autumn leaves.

element, in gloss, means air.

314. **fire flags.** Lightning.

317-24. The original reading was:

> The coming wind doth roar more loud;
> The sails do sigh like sedge:
> The rain pours down from one black cloud
> And the Moon is at its edge.
>
> Hark! hark! the thick black cloud is cleft,
> And the Moon is at its side. . . .

333. **it had.** Older idiom for " it would have been."

337. **'gan work.** Did work. A Spenserianism.

345. This line takes the reader back to the opening of IV.

358. **a-dropping.** Archaic, as *a-hunting, a-fishing*.

362. **jargoning.** Song of birds. The word is from Chaucer. Here it takes a slight accent on the final syllable.

Notes on the Ancient Mariner

This stanza prepares skillfully for the reintroduction of land scenes. It comes beautifully and quietly after the end of the song of the spirits.

369. **like of.** Elliptical for "like that of. The "hidden brook" may have been suggested by one known to Coleridge and Wordsworth in the Nether Stowey region, and mentioned several times by them in their poetry.

372. These stanzas appeared between 372 and 374 in the original text. They were omitted in 1800.

> Listen, O listen, thou Wedding-Guest!
> 'Marinere! thou hast thy will:
> 'For that, which comes out of thine eye, doth make
> 'My body and soul to be still.'
>
> Never sadder tale was told
> To a man of woman born:
> Sadder and wiser thou wedding-guest!
> Thou'lt rise to morrow morn.
>
> Never sadder tale was heard
> By a man of woman born:
> The Marineres all return'd to work
> As silent as beforne.
>
> The Marineres all 'gan pull the ropes,
> But look at me they n'old;
> Thought I, I am as thin as air—
> They cannot me behold.

There are many changes in the movement along here, echoic and suitable as elsewhere; for example, 373-76, 389-92.

392. **swound.** See note on l. 62.

daemon, in gloss. Guardian spirit or tutelary genius. The same word as *demon*, but having not necessarily malevolent implication.

407. **honey dew.** Sugar exuded from leaves. Used also in *Kubla Khan*.

This part ends in calm, and again with a reference to the albatross.

VI. This part opens with the antiphonal voices of the polar spirits. It tells of the miraculous homeward voyage of the Mariner.

423. **or . . . or.** *Either . . . or*, as in Shakespeare.

428. **slow and slow.** A repetition that arouses attention and curiosity.

431. Notice the archaic effect of *a ge*

Notes on the Ancient Mariner

435. **charnel dungeon.** Dungeon is a death house.

442–46. The following stanza was omitted at this point in *Sibylline Leaves*:

> And in its time the spell was snapt
> And I could move my een:
> I look'd far-forth but little saw
> Of what might else be seen.

459. **welcoming.** Given a slight final accent, in the ballad fashion.

460. **Swiftly, swiftly flew the ship.** The effect of this line seems to echo that of a line in the ballad, *Barbara Allen's Cruelty*:

> And slowly, slowly she rose up.

466. The landmarks appear again, this time in inverse order. The effect of the Mariner's recognition makes itself felt in the verse form.

467. **countrie.** With final accent, as in the ballads. Compare this stanza from one of the *Robin Hood* ballads:

> There sat a yeoman by his side;
> 'Tell mee, sweet page,' said hee,
> 'What is thy business or the cause,
> So far in the North Country?'

475. These stanzas originally appeared between lines 475–80:

> The moonlight bay was white all o'er,
> Till rising from the same,
> Full many shapes, that shadows were,
> Like as of torches came.
>
> A little distance from the prow
> Those dark-red shadows were;
> But soon I saw that my own flesh
> Was red as in a glare.
>
> I turn'd my head in fear and dread,
> And by the holy rood,
> The bodies had advanc'd, and now
> Before the mast they stood.
>
> They lifted up their stiff right arms,
> They held them straight and tight;
> And each right-arm burnt like a torch,
> A torch that's borne upright.
> Their stony eye-balls glitter'd on
> In the red and smoky light.

Notes on the Ancient Mariner

> I pray'd and turn'd my head away
> Forth looking as before.
> There was no breeze upon the bay,
> No wave against the shore.

489. **rood.** Cross.

490. **seraph man.** Angelic spirit. Compare the manner in which the ships are guided home in the letter of Bishop Paulinus, Introduction, p. 23. This picture of the seraph spirits standing on the dead bodies is one of the most memorable in the poem.

494. **signals.** Much as vessels at night summon a pilot by a flare.

503–04. Between these stanzas originally occurred six lines:

> Then vanish'd all the lovely lights;
> The bodies rose anew:
> With silent pace, each to his place,
> Came back the ghastly crew.
> The wind, that shade nor motion made,
> On me alone it blew.

509. **hermit.** A favorite figure, in early nineteenth century literature. Most of the hermits of the Romantic poets cross the mediæval conception with that of the 'solitary,' or voluntary social exile, who was so admired a figure in poetry after Rousseau. So in Wordsworth's *Tintern Abbey*. Coleridge's hermit is purely mediæval, of course.

512. **shrieve.** Old form of *shrive*.

513. The last reference to the albatross.

VII. Coleridge gives his poem seven parts. Compare the "Seven days, seven nights," of 261 and the "seven days drowned" of 552.

As the poem closes, the scene is again on land.

521–22. **moss . . . stump.** Again commonplace words, here poetically effective. There were many moss-covered stumps of oak in the Nether Stowey region through which Coleridge and the Wordsworths walked.

523. **skiff-boat.** See note on l. 41.

524. **trow.** Old word for *believe*.

532. **were.** Imperfect rhyme for *cheer* and *sere*. This is the only "overflow" stanza in the poem.

535. **ivy tod.** *Tod* is an old word, meaning bush or heavy growth. It is used by Spenser. The hermit's simile for the sails is protracted through six lines, and rather overweights the passage.

Notes on the Ancient Mariner

540. **afeard.** Compare *Macbeth*, I, iii, 96.

545. **sound.** This marks the approach of the climax, which comes in 548-49, when the ship disappears, in the presence of the Pilot and his boy. The ebb begins in 556 onward. The ship was never to be brought to land.

560-70. Coleridge shows the effect which the Mariner's days of torment had left upon him by showing the effect which his dread has upon others.

575. **agony.** Has a slight final accent. So *company*, l. 604.

The Mariner's explanation is much more effective, at the end, than it would have been, had it been given at the beginning.

Other celebrated wanderers of romance are the Wandering Jew of mediæval legend, and the fabled mariner, the Flying Dutchman.

582-85. Originally:—

> Since then, at some uncertain hour,
> Now ofttimes and now fewer,
> That anguish comes and makes me tell
> My ghastly aventure.

Aventure is from Chaucer. Nearly every discarded passage contains some striking older word, or older form.

591. Again sound, marked by change in stanzaic form—this time from the breaking-up of the wedding feast—brings interruption and change. It helps the unity of the poem that it ends, as it began, with the wedding feast.

623. **forlorn.** Deprived of.

NOTES ON CHRISTABEL

THE preface to the 1816 edition contained the following passage: " . . . the meter of Christabel is not, properly speaking, irregular, though it may seem so from its being founded on a new principle: namely, that of counting in each line the accents, not the syllables. Though the latter may vary from seven to twelve, yet in each line the accents will be found to be only four. Nevertheless, this occasional variation in the number of syllables is not introduced wantonly, or for the mere ends of convenience, but in correspondence with some transition in the nature of the imagery or passion."

Coleridge's "new principle" of composing by accents rather than by syllables was the governing principle of Old English poetry, which had four accents to the line, but no fixed number of syllables. Similar prosody is found in Spenser's *The Shepherd's Calendar*. The February Eclogue has four accents to the line but feet not of fixed length. But the musical effect of Coleridge's verse is different.

1. **castle clock.** Clocks which struck the hour were an invention of the middle ages. When Shakespeare introduces them into *Julius Cæsar*, they are anachronistic; but they are not in this poem.

3. **Tu-whit!—Tu-whoo!** Used in one of the lyrics in Shakespeare's *Love's Labor Lost*.

> Then nightly sings the staring owl
> Tu-whit, tu-who! a merry note,

12-13. The howling of the mastiff is premonitory of evil.

14-15. Coleridge's frequent use of question and answer in *Christabel* may reflect the usage of the ballads. Compare 26, 57-58, etc.

21. **a month before the month of May.** April and May are the favorite months of mediæval poets. So Chaucer.

54. This is the line borrowed by Scott in his *Lay of the Last Minstrel*.

58. **damsel.** A favorite term for a young woman of gentle birth, in the mediæval romances.

66. **I guess.** Used by Chaucer, as in his ʊ. ˊ ˗ l. 82. Now often called an Americanism.

69. A frequent mediæval exrl·

Notes on Christabel

80. **Geraldine.** Coleridge rhymes this name with *wine, pine, divine*, ll. 105, 139, 191, 205, etc. Its last syllable is usually pronounced as rhyming with *seen, mien, etc.*

84. **palfrey.** A saddle or road horse, suitable for ladies.

85. **wind.** In poetical usage, a rhyme for *behind, find*, etc. The pronunciation with shortened vowel, now in standard usage, seems to have been extended to the noun from compounds like *windmill, windbreak*, where the shortening is more logical.

87. **amain.** With full force. Archaic.

92. **I wis.** I know. The old adverb, *y-wis, i-wis*, German *gewiss*, was confused in Coleridge's day with the related verb, *wot, wist*, German *weiss, wuste*, and the prefix, *y-*, older *ge-*, mistaken for the personal pronoun. There is properly no such verb form as *wis*. Coleridge uses *you wis* in *Alice du Clos*. Both the proper adverbial and the spurious verbal usage are found in the old ballads.

129. It is difficult for Geraldine to cross the threshold—possibly from weariness, but more likely because it has been blessed.

belike. Probably, perhaps. Archaic.

141. Nor is she able to praise the Virgin.

148. **angry moan.** As though the mastiff were conscious of a supernatural presence.

152. **scritch.** Screech. A rare or dialectal form.

159. Even the fire is aware of the supernatural presence.

162. **boss.** The central projection of the shield.

171. Other instances of inner rhyme occur ll. 306, 317, 329, 528, 561, 570, etc.

175–183. This description of Geraldine's chamber has been greatly admired. Keats was perhaps influenced by it in his description of Madeline's chamber in *St. Agnes' Eve*.

205. Geraldine seems to exercise the spirit of Christabel's mother. Or is this too hallucination?

217. **wildered.** Poetic for *bewildered*.

221. The glittering eyes associated with serpents.

225. **countrée.** The form and accent of the word in ballad usage. See note on *The Ancient Mariner*, l. 467.

249. **cincture.** Poetic for *girdle*.

252–54. What this disfigurement is, or whether it really exists, we are not told. In older romantic literature, as *The Faerie Queene* or the ballads, are many stories of transformations of human beings into other living creatures, or *vice versa*. There is generally some mark of betrayal, or some period when the real form is wholly or partly resumed.

264. **wel-a-day.** Alas. Poetic or archaic.

266. Christabel is hypnotized, as it were.

Notes on Christabel

271. Short rhymed stanzas frequently appear at the end of divisions in the older metrical romances. See also 632–35.
288. **bale.** Evil. Archaic.
294. **I wis.** See note on l. 92.
306. **tairn.** Scottish form of *tarn*, a small mountain lake.
310. **fell.** A moor, or down.
320. **hermitess.** There were professional hermits in the middle ages, but Coleridge's hermitess is a poetical fancy.
332. **matin bell.** Calling to the morning religious service.
339. **sacristan.** The officer in charge of the church utensils or movables; sometimes a sexton.
341. **beads.** Prayers. The name was later applied to the balls on the rosary, used for telling prayers.
344. **Bratha Head.** The river Brathay flows into Lake Windermere. Coleridge prefers the old spelling, Wyndermere.
350. **Langdale Pike.** Pike means peak, or pointed hill.
351. **Dungeon-ghyll.** A *ghyll* is a ravine with a stream running through it. Wordsworth speaks of Greenhead-*ghyll* in Michael. There is a Loch Dungeon in Southern Scotland.
354. **t'other.** Archaic contraction of *the other*. *Tother* is found in Shakespeare.
359. **Borodale.** There is a Borrowdale valley, in the English Lake region.
364. **vestments.** Poetic for garments.
396. **presence-room.** The room where great personages receive guests.
408–426. This poignant passage about friendship, lines from which were prefixed by Lord Byron to his poem *Farewell*, sounds more modern than mediæval, and it seems somewhat out of connection, in the context.
426. **been.** A rhyme for *ween*, in British English. Spenser rhymes *been* with both *seen* and *in*, etc. The shortened vowel came to America with the colonists, while the older form remained in England.
433. A favorite mediæval oath. It also took the shortened forms *zounds, swounds* (God's wouñds), etc. **Jesu.** Poetical form, really the vocative of *Jesus*.
440. **recreant.** Yielding, cowardly.
441. **tourney.** Variant of *tournament*.
445. **kenned.** Knew.
455–56. The narrator's parenthetical interruption, in the manner of the old verse romances.
459. Again the dread suggestion.
484. **bard.** A stock figure in the older romantic literature.
493. **Irthing flood . . . Knorren Moor . . . Halegarth**

Notes on Christabel

Wood. These references add to the definite localization of Part II on North English soil.

498 ff. Scott's *Young Lochinvar* sounds as though he were echoing the prosody of this passage.

517. **again.** A good rhyme for Tryermaine, in British English

527 The poet makes use of the premonitory or allegorical dream, a stock device in older French and English literature; much used, for example, by Chaucer.

582–585. The serpent association is made yet more specific.

591. Christabel is again as though hypnotized.

656. This conclusion has no apparent relation to the rest of the poem. The three extant manuscripts of the poem do not contain it. It was sent to Southey, May 6, 1801. Since the Second Part was written in 1800, the Conclusion was perhaps of later composition.

NOTES ON KUBLA KHAN

1. **Xanadu.** A region in Tartary. Coleridge's *Xanadu* is a dream-reminiscence, or intentional modification of *Xaindu*. The passage from *Purchas his Pilgrimage* (1614, second edition) Bk. IV, chapter xiii, from which Coleridge quotes from memory, runs: "In Xaindu did Cublai Can build a stately Pallace, encompassing sixteene miles of plaine ground with a wall, wherein are fertile Meddowes, pleasant Springs, delightful Streames, and all sorts of beasts, chase, and game, and in the middest thereof a sumptuous house of pleasure." The spelling of the traveller Marco Polo (1254-1323) is *Chandu*.

khan. A title of the ruling monarchs of Tartary. The Khan Kubla was a grandson of the great Gengis Khan of history, the founder of the Tartar empire, the Cambynskan of Chaucer's *The Squire's Tale*, and the "Cambuscan bold" of Milton's *Il Penseroso*.

3. **Alph.** This name seems to have been suggested by the Alpheus, the chief river of the Pelopennesus. See Ovid, *Metamorphoses*, Book V, ll. 572-641.

Robert Louis Stevenson, in an article entitled "Some Technical Elements of Style in Literature," originally published in *The Contemporary Review*, April, 1885, analyzes the pervading sound-elements in this passage by means of the key-letters in the margin:

In Xanadu did Kubla Khan	(KANDL)
A stately pleasure-dome decree,	(KDLSR)
Where Alph the sacred river ran	(KANDLSR)
Through caverns measureless to man,	(KANLSR)
Down to a sunless sea.	(NDLS)

Stevenson discusses some of the more subtle effects of vowel and consonant color, as appearing in both prose and verse.

16. This line was used by Byron as a motto for his *Heaven and Earth*, published in 1823.

40. **dulcimer.** Ancient musical instrument. Dulcimers, locally called "dulcimores," are still used in the Cumberland Mountains of the Southern United States, though they have been almost replaced by the fiddle and the banjo. They have descended from Elizabethan England as the traditional accompaniment of mountain ballad-singing. They are made of curved bos black walnut, thinly planed, and look not unlike a

necked violins. They are strung with three strings, sometimes of gut, usually of wire; occasionally a bow is used, but often they are plucked by the hands. "The tonal quality is very light—a ghastly disembodied sort of music." W. A. Bradley, "Song-Balletts and Devil's Ditties," *Harper's Magazine*, 130, 901-914, 1915.

41. Mount Abora. Professor Lane Cooper, in an article entitled "The Abyssinian Paradise in Coleridge and Milton," *Modern Philology*, 1906, p. 327, suggests that this mount was suggested by the Mount Amara of legend. There is no Mount Abora in Abyssinia, but Purchas, whose book Coleridge was reading, devotes a whole chapter to "Of the Hill Amara." Professor Cooper thinks of *Kubla Khan* as a "vision of the terrestrial paradise." Compare Milton, *Paradise Lost*, IV, ll, 280-86, 540-49. The reference to the Tartar paradise at the opening leads the poet to compare it with the Abyssinian, in the middle of the poem, and there is a suggestion of the bewitched enclosures of the Old Man of the Mountain (Purchas, 428) at the end. Or the poem, he thinks, might be a dream of the false, rather than the terrestrial, paradise, since it admits demoniacal love to its "holy" precincts. "It reads like an arras of reminiscences from several accounts of natural or enchanted parks, and from various descriptions of that elusive and danger-fraught garden which mysterious geographers have studied to locate from Florida to Cathay."

Some of the reappearing essentials, Professor Cooper points out, of the conception of the terrestrial paradise are the fountain with outpouring rills, the symmetrical mountain, the disappearing sacred river, and the wall enclosing all. Compare Book IV of *Paradise Lost*.

Here are a few excerpts from Purchas's chapter:

"The hill Amara . . . is situate as the . . . . center of their Empire, vnder the Equinoctiall line, where the Sun may take his best view thereof, as not encountering in all his long iourny with the like Theatre, wherein the Graces & Muses are actors, no place more graced with Natures store . . . the Sunne himself so in loue with the sight, that the first & last thing he vieweth in all those parts is this hill . . . some taking this for the place of our Fore-fathers Paradise. . . .

It is situate in a great Plaine largely extending itselfe every way, without other hill in the same for the space of 30 leagues, the forme thereof round and circular, the height such, that it is a daies worke to ascend from the foot to the top. . . . It is above twenty leagues in circuit compassed with a wall on top, *well wrought*, that neither man nor beast in chase may falle

Notes on Kubla Khan

down . . . yeelding also a pleasant spring which passeth through all that Plaine . . . and making a Lake, whence issueth a River. . . . The way vp to it [the top] is cut out within the Rocke, not with staires, but ascending by little and little. . . . Halfe way vp is a faire and spacious Hall cut out of the same rocke, with three windowes. . . . There are no Cities on the top, but palaces, standing by themselves, in number four and thirtie, spacious, sumptuous, and beautifull." . . .

Specific localization, or logical interpretation, are not essential, however, for the appreciation of the poem.

47. **caves of ice.** See also 1, 36. Coleridge's sunny dome and caves of ice, which have puzzled many readers, may have been suggested, thinks Professor Cooper, by the sunlit and symmetrical hill of Mt. Amara; though why "of ice" is hard to understand, unless the rock was thought of as of marble or alabaster. Professor Bronson thinks that the phrase may have been used to suggest "welcome coolness in a tropical climate."

NOTES ON FRANCE: AN ODE

This poem was written in February, 1798. It was first published under the title *Recantation: An Ode*, in the *Morning Post*, April 16, 1798. Its present name was substituted when it was reprinted. In 1798 Napoleon was conducting a successful war against Italy, and menaced Switzerland. The struggle of France for freedom seemed to be turning into an attempt to wrest its liberties from the rest of Europe. In 1799 Napoleon seized the government of France by a *coup d'état*, and became First Consul of the Republic. A few years later he became Emperor. The Revolution and the Reign of Terror were followed by Napoleonic imperialism. Wordsworth and Coleridge began as radicals, in strong sympathy with the Revolution, but their radicalism was changed into conservatism following the development of events in France. To the original *Morning Post* version was prefixed the following editorial note:

"The following excellent ode will be in unison with the feelings of every friend to liberty and foe to oppression; of all who, admiring the French Revolution, detest and deplore the conduct of France toward Switzerland. It is very satisfactory to find so zealous and steady an advocate for freedom as Mr. Coleridge concur with us in condemning the conduct of France toward the Swiss Cantons. Indeed his concurrence is not singular; we know of no friend to liberty who is not of his opinion. What we most admire is the *avowal* of his sentiments, and public censure of the unprincipled and atrocious conduct of France. The poem itself is written with great energy. The second, third, and fourth stanzas contain some of the most vigorous lines that we have ever read."

The ode was reprinted in the *Morning Post* in 1802, when the relations of France and Switzerland again gave it strong current interest. The following argument was prefixed:—

"*First Stanza*. An invocation to those objects in nature, the contemplation of which had inspired the poet with a devotional love of Liberty. *Second Stanza*. The exultation of the poet at the commencement of the French Revolution, and his unqualified abhorrence of the Alliance against the Republic. *Third Stanza*. The blasphemies and horrors during the domination of the Terrorists regarded by the poet as a transient storm, and as the natural consequence of the former despotism and of the foul *superstition* of Popery. Reason, indeed, began to suggest many *apprehensions*; yet still the poet struggled to retain the hope that

Notes on France: An Ode

France would make conquests by no other means than by presenting to the observation of Europe a people more happy and better instructed than under any other forms of government. *Fourth Stanza.* Switzerland, and the poet's recantation. *Fifth Stanza.* An address to Liberty, in which the poet expresses his conviction that those feelings and that grand *ideal* of Freedom which the mind attains by its contemplation of its individual nature, and of the sublime surrounding objects (see Stanza the First) do not belong to men as a society, nor can possibly be either gratified or realized, under any form of human government; but belong to the individual man, so far as he is pure, and inflamed with the love and adoration of God in nature."

I. In this first stanza, sometimes called its "famous exordium," the poet calls upon the clouds, ocean-waves, woods, sun, sky, to testify to his constant love of liberty. Coleridge does not define the liberty which he has in mind as 'his poem opens. Ideas of liberty varied for the early nineteenth century poets. To Wordsworth, freedom was something political, external. Especially it was freedom from a foreign political yoke, possibly also, freedom from an autocrat or tyrant at home. The heroes of his "Sonnets Dedicated to Liberty" are the national political or military heroes, like Pitt, Wellington, Nelson. He had no special thought of individual liberty, such as liberty of conduct, or of the pen. Shelley's conception was wider-ranging, and so was Byron's. With Shelley liberty is not something to be attained by a change of government or by a military campaign; for there may be spiritual bondage under political freedom. Shelley and Byron desired not only political liberty but liberty of thought, speech, action.

II. **embattled by a wizard's wand.** Like fiends summoned by the wand of an enchanter. The poet refers to the European alliance against the young French republic.

pæans. Songs of joy, triumph, praise, or thanksgiving, among the ancient Greeks.

III. **Blasphemy's loud scream.** Coleridge has in mind scenes like those at a celebration of a Feast of Reason in 1793, when a Goddess of Reason, an actress, was borne in triumph to the altar of Notre Dame cathedral and enthroned there. This was when the Reign of Terror was at its worst.

IV. **Helvetia.** Latin name for Switzerland. Compare the *Helvetii* who occupied this region in Cæsar's day.

V. Coleridge returns to the clouds, winds, waves of the beginning. In communion with these he finds peace; only here is true freedom to be attained by the human spirit. One critic remarks that the doctrine at the close of the ode approaches "*political despair.*"

QUESTIONS

THE ANCIENT MARINER

GENERAL QUESTIONS

How did the poem come to be composed? What are the author's chief indebtednesses for the materials entering into it? What is the setting and its relation to the narrative? Describe the structure of the poem. What are the chief events in each division? Show how each part ends in a climax. How is the story made to move with such rapidity? Are we completely out of touch, during the narrative, with the real world and with the land? Has the poem human interest, or is this element lacking? Name and describe the major and minor characters. Is interest in them as individuals a chief thing? Is the narrative to be localized in time and place? For land scenes? For sea scenes? What elements entering into it are mediæval? What modern? What supernatural figures or agencies in the poem? Which leave the more permanent impression on you, the natural or the supernatural elements? Are you more impressed by the moral, or by the story, or by the way in which the two are interwoven? How important is the moral?

Make a list of archaic words. Why are they used? Make a list of simple words used with especial force or vividness. Give examples of alliteration; of onomatapœia; of figures of speech. What is the usual stanza form? Point out variations from it. What are the elements which the poem owes to the popular ballad?

THE NARRATIVE

Part I. What characters are introduced? How do you imagine them to look? What are the events of this part? What are its scenes? Why did the Mariner kill the albatross? How does the story begin? Would it be better if the author had begun with more description?

Part II. What is developed in the narrative in this part regarding the voyage of the ship and the relation of the Mariner to his comrades? What are its scenes? Do you think that all the details are to be accepted as actually happening or as imag*ined by the Mariner?*

Questions on The Ancient Mariner

Part III. What are the events or incidents in this part and the effect on the characters? What are the feelings of the Mariner? Why did the sailors die? Why not the Mariner also? What scene do you remember most vividly?

Part IV. What events or incidents in this division? What descriptions or pictures? What turning point in the narrative? Why does the albatross fall from the Mariner's neck?

Part V. Summarize the happenings of this part as affecting the Mariner. What are the pictures? The contrasts? What do the voices heard by the Mariner represent?

Part VI. What occupies this part? Why are the voices continued? What part do they play in the narrative? Has the Mariner's penance ended? Why is he so happy? Does any picture stand out with especial vividness?

Part VII. How does the narrative end? What purpose is served by the introduction of the Hermit in this part? What happened to the Pilot's boy? Would you expect the ship to come to shore like an ordinary ship? Why does the Mariner tell his story to the Wedding Guest instead of to another? Is it better that the Mariner tells the reason for his narration as the poem closes instead of as it opens?

TOPICS FOR DISCUSSION OR REPORT

How does Coleridge give the "illusion of reality" to his strange narrative? What elements in the poem give it the effect of a dream? Describe the coming and going of the phantom ship. Give an account of the pictures of the sea. Give an account of the color and light effects, the sunlight pictures, the moonlight pictures, the ice picture, etc. Indicate the supernatural events in the poem. Indicate the stages of the Mariner's penance. Show the geographical course of the Mariner's ship from its departure until its return. Summarize the narrative, observing the division into parts. What are the moral teachings of the poem and how or where they are implied? Is the Mariner justly punished for killing the albatross? Indicate the succession of nature scenes in the poem. Show how the story is told by pictures. What are the relations of the Mariner and the sailors? Follow the relation of the Ancient Mariner to the Wedding Guest. Point out strong contrasts, in the poem, of movement or sound.

Christabel

GENERAL QUESTIONS AND TOPICS FOR DISCUSSION

Do you remember the poem by its narrative, by its characters, or by its scenes, atmosphere, and unique melodies? Enumerate and discuss the characters of the poem. How do you imagine them to have looked? Contrast the traits of Christabel and Geraldine. Point out the supernatural elements or agencies in the poem. Describe the castle and some of the details of feudal life presented. Has the poem moral meaning beyond picturing a conflict between innocence and evil?

What does Coleridge say were his principles of metrical composition in *Christabel?* Analyze the metrical movement of a few paragraphs. Show how Coleridge introduces metrical variation corresponding to changes in the action or the feeling. Find examples of alternate rhymes instead of couplet rhymes; of triple rhymes; of inner rhymes.

THE NARRATIVE

Part I. How is the reader prepared for the reception of strange and incredible things? Into how many scenes does the first part fall? What are they? Was Geraldine a sorceress, or does she only seem so to Christabel, or does the poet tell us with certainty? Point out omens of the malign character of her presence.

Part II. What scene or scenes in this part? Show wherein it is more definitely localized than Part I, although fewer descriptive details are given. Does the localization help? What new characters in this part? What is the significance of Bracy's dream? Why the Baron's anger at his daughter?

Does the poem contain any clues as to how it might have been concluded? Do you regret that Coleridge did not finish the poem? Show stage by stage Geraldine's relation to and influence upon Christabel. How did she exercise her power over Christabel? Are her motives clear? How is the mother linked with the story?

KUBLA KHAN

What is Coleridge's account of the composition of the poem? What succession of scenes or dream pictures in the poem? Are they connected? Do you find logical sequence? Indicate some of the details of landscape suggested. Are there suggestions of *sound* as well as pictorial suggestion? Point out lines where the prosodic effect is accelerated or lightened; lines where it is purposely retarded or made harsh. Point out instances of alliteration, of assonance, or of recurrence of the "key" vowel sound. Has the poem human interest? Has it effect on the mind, or on the feeling? How far is the impression made by it oral? How far associational? Try to distinguish the quality of its music from that of *The Ancient Mariner* and *Christabel*.

FRANCE: AN ODE

I. What is the poet's invocation in this stanza? What do you think he has in mind by "freedom" in this stanza? Is it political? Personal? Spiritual? Is it inner or external? Study the musical structure of the verse paragraph. Show how a climax is reached. Is the metrical scheme the same in all the stanzas?

II. How did the poet feel in the earlier days of the French Revolution? Where were his sympathies? What was his feeling toward England, and why?

III. What was his attitude during the Reign of Terror? What did he expect of France? What did he think would be the outcome?

IV. Explain his revulsion of feeling in this stanza. Where are his sympathies now, and why?

V. What stage has he reached at the end? Where does he seek refuge? Is his conception of liberty the same as at the beginning? Is it inner or external? How does he seem to feel regarding human society? Does the close of the poem leave you content?

Is a theme of strong contemporary interest, like that of the ode, likely to help or to detract from the permanent interest of a poem?

APPENDIX

COLERIDGE AT CHRIST'S HOSPITAL

COME back into memory, like as thou wert in the day-spring of thy fancies, with hope like a fiery column before thee—the dark pillar not yet turned—Samuel Taylor Coleridge—Logician, Metaphysician, Bard!—How have I seen the casual passer through the Cloisters stand still entranced with admiration (while he weighed the disproportion between the *speech* and the *garb* of the young Mirandula), to hear thee unfold, in thy deep and sweet intonations the mysteries of Jamblichus, or Plotinus (for even in those years thou waxedst not pale at such philosophic draughts), or reciting Homer in his Greek, or Pindar—while the walls of the old Grey Friars re-echoed to the accents of the *inspired charity boy!* Many were the "wit combats" (to dally awhile with the words of old Fuller), between him and C. V. Le G——, "which two I behold like a Spanish great galleon, and an English man-of-war; Master Coleridge, like the former, was built far higher in learning, solid, but slow in his performances. C. V. L., with the English man-of-war, lesser in bulk, but lighter in sailing, could turn with all tides, tack about and take advantage of all winds, by the quickness of his wit and invention."[1]

WILLIAM HAZLITT ON COLERIDGE

. . . It was in January of 1798 that I rose one morning before daylight, to walk ten miles in the mud, to hear this celebrated person preach. Never, the longest day I have to live, shall I have such another walk as this cold, raw, comfortless one, in the winter of the year 1798. . . . When I got there, the organ was playing the 100th psalm, and when it was done, Mr. Coleridge rose and gave out his text, "And he went up into the mountain to pray, himself, alone." As he gave out this text, his voice "rose like a steam of rich distilled perfumes," and when he came to the two last words, which he pronounced loud, deep, and distinct, it seemed to me, who was then young, as if the sounds had echoed from the bottom of the human heart, and as if that prayer might have floated in solemn silence through the universe. The idea of St. John came into my mind, "of one crying in the wilderness, who had his loins girt about, and whose

[1] From Charles Lamb's *Christ's Hospital Five-and-Thirty Years Ago*, 1813.

Appendix

food was locusts and wild honey." The preacher then launched into his subject, like an eagle dallying with the wind. The sermon was upon peace and war; upon church and state—not their alliance but their separation—on the spirit of the world and the spirit of Christianity, not as the same, but as opposed to one another! He talked of those who had "inscribed the cross of Christ on banners dripping with human gore." He made a poetical and pastoral excursion—and to show the fatal effects of war, drew a striking contrast between the simple shepherd boy, driving his team afield, or sitting under the hawthorne, piping to his flock, "as though he should never be old," and the same poor country lad, crimped, kidnapped, brought into town, made drunk at an alehouse, turned into a wretched drummer boy, with his hair sticking on end with powder and pomatum, a long cue at his back, and tricked out in the loathsome finery of the profession of blood. . . . And for myself, I could not have been more delighted if I had heard the music of the spheres. Poetry and Philosophy had met together. Truth and Genius had embraced, under the eye and with the sanction of Religion. This was even beyond my hopes. I returned home well satisfied. The sun that was still labouring pale and wan through the sky, obscured by thick mists, seemed an emblem of the good cause; and the cold dank drops of dew, that hung half-melted on the beard of the thistle, had something genial and refreshing in them; for there was a spirit of hope and youth in all nature, that turned everything into good. . . .

. . . . It was a fine morning in the middle of winter, and he talked the whole way. . . . In digressing, in dilating, in passing from subject to subject, he appeared to me to float in air, to slide on ice. . . . I observed that he continually crossed me on the way by shifting from one side of the footpath to the other. This struck me as an odd movement; but I did not at that time connect it with any instability of purpose or involuntary change of principle, as I have done since. He seemed unable to keep on in a straight line. . . . He was the first poet I had known, and he certainly answered to that inspired name. I had heard a great deal of his powers of conversation and was not disappointed. In fact, I never met with anything at all like them either before or since. I could easily credit the accounts which were circulated of his holding forth to a large party of gentlemen and ladies, an evening or two before, on the Berkeleian Theory, when he made the whole material universe look like a transparency of fine words; and another story (which I believe he has somewhere told himself) of his being asked to a party at Birmingham, of his smoking tobacco and going to sleep after dinner on a sofa, where the company found him, to their no

Appendix

small surprise, which was increased to wonder when he started up of a sudden, and, rubbing his eyes, looked about him, and launched into a three-hours' description of the third heaven, of which he had had a dream, very different from Mr. Southey's *Vision of Judgment*. . . .

. . . There is a chaunt in the recitation of both Coleridge and Wordsworth, which acts as a spell upon the hearer, and disarms the judgment. Perhaps they have deceived themselves by making habitual use of this ambiguous accompaniment. Coleridge's manner is more full, animated, and varied; Wordsworth's more equable, sustained, and internal. The one might be termed more *dramatic,* the other more *lyrical.* Coleridge has told me that he himself liked to compose in walking over uneven ground, or breaking through the straggling branches of a copse-wood; whereas Wordsworth always wrote (if he could) walking up and down a straight gravel walk, or in some spot where the continuity of his verse met with no collateral interruption.[2]

First Impressions of Coleridge

He is a wonderful man. His conversation teems with soul, mind, and spirit. Then he is so benevolent, so good tempered and cheerful, and, like William, interests himself so much about every little trifle. At first I thought him very plain, that is, for about three minutes: he is pale, thin, has a wide mouth, thick lips, and not very good teeth, longish, loose-growing, half-curling, rough black hair. But, if you hear him speak for five minutes, you think no more of them. His eye is large and full, and not very dark, but grey—such an eye as would receive from a heavy soul the dullest expression; but it speaks every emotion of his animated mind; it has more of 'the poet's eye in a fine frenzy rolling' than I ever witnessed. He has fine dark eyebrows, and an overhanging forehead.[3]

Coleridge's Last Days

Coleridge sat on the brow of Highgate Hill, in those years, looking down on London and its smoke tumult like a sage escaped from the inanity of life's battle, attracting toward him the thoughts of innumerable brave souls still engaged there. His express contributions to poetry, philosophy, or any specific province of human literature or enlightenment had been small and sadly intermittent; but he had, especially among young inquiring men, a higher than literary, a kind of prophetic or magician character. He was thought to hold—he alone in England—the

[2] From *My First Acquaintance with Poets.* 1823.
[3] *Dorothy* Wordsworth, *Memoirs of Wordsworth,* I, 99.

Appendix

key of German and other Transcendentalisms; knew the sublime secret of believing by the 'reason' what the 'understanding' had been obliged to fling out as incredible; and could still, after Hume and Voltaire had done their best and worst with him, profess himself an orthodox Christian, and say and point to the Church of England, with its singular old rubrics and surplices at Allhallowtide, *Esto perpetua*. A sublime man, who alone in those dark days had saved his crown of spiritual manhood, escaping from the black materialisms and revolutionary deluges with 'God, Freedom, Immortality' still his; a king of men. The practical intellects of the world did not much heed him, or carelessly reckoned him a metaphysical dreamer; but to the rising spirits of the young generation he had this dusky sublime character, and sat there as a kind of Magus, girt in mystery and enigma; his Dodona oak-grove (Mr. Gillman's house at Highgate) whispering strange things, uncertain whether oracles or jargons.

The Gillmans did not encourage much company or excitation of any sort round their sage; nevertheless, access to him, if a youth did reverently wish it, was not difficult. He would stroll about the pleasant garden with you, sit in the pleasant rooms of the place—perhaps take you to his own peculiar room, high up, with a rearward view, which was the chief view of all. A really charming outlook in fine weather. Close at hand wide sweeps of flowing leafy gardens, their few houses mostly hidden, the very chimney-pots veiled under blossoming umbrage, flowed gloriously down hill; gloriously issuing in wide-tufted undulating plain country, rich in all charms of field and town. Waving blooming country of the brightest green, dotted all over with handsome villas, handsome groves crossed by roads and human traffic, here inaudible, or heard only as a musical hum; and behind all swam, under olive-tinted haze, the illimitable limitary ocean of London, with its domes and steeples definite in the sun, big Paul's and the many memories attached to it hanging high over all. Nowhere of its kind could you see a grander prospect on a bright summer day, with the set of the air going southward—southward, and so draping with the city smoke not *you* but the city.

Here for hours would Coleridge talk concerning all conceivable or inconceivable things; and liked nothing better than to have an intelligent, or, failing that, even a silent and patient human listener. He distinguished himself to all that ever heard him as at least the most surprising talker extant in this world—and to some small minority, by no means to all, as the most excellent.

The good man—he was now getting old, toward sixty perhaps, and gave you the idea of a life that had been full of sufferings; a life heavy-laden, half-vanquished, still swimming painfully in seas of manifold physical and other bewilderment.

Appendix

Brow and head were round and of massive weight, but the face was flabby and irresolute. The deep eyes, of a light hazel, were as full of sorrow as of inspiration; confused pain looked mildly from them, as in a kind of mild astonishment. The whole figure and air, good and amiable otherwise, might be called flabby and irresolute; expressive of weakness under possibility of strength. He hung loosely on his limbs, with knees bent, and stooping attitude; in walking he rather shuffled than decisively stept; and a lady once remarked that he never could fix which side of the garden-walk would suit him best, but continually shifted, cork-screw fashion, and kept trying both; a heavy-laden, high-aspiring, and surely much-suffering man. His voice, naturally soft and good, had contracted itself into a plaintive snuffle and sing-song; he spoke as if preaching—you could have said preaching earnestly and almost hopelessly the weightiest things. I still recollect his 'object' and 'subject,' terms of continual recurrence in the Kantean province; and how he sang and snuffled them into 'om-m-ject' and 'sum-m-m-ject,' with a kind of solemn shake or quaver as he rolled along. No talk in his century or in any other could be more surprising.*

COLERIDGE'S CONVERSATION

To pass an entire day with Coleridge was a marvellous change indeed [from the talk of daily life]. It was a Sabbath past expression, deep and tranquil and serene. You came to a man who had travelled in many countries and in critical times; who had seen and felt the world in most of its ranks and in many of its vicissitudes and weaknesses; one to whom, with a reasonable allowance as to technical details, all science was, in a most extraordinary degree, familiar. Throughout a long-drawn summer's day would this man talk to you in low, equable, but clear and musical tones concerning things human and divine; marshalling all history, harmonizing all experiment, probing the depths of your consciousness, and revealing visions of glory and terror to the imagination; but pouring withal such floods of light upon the mind that you might for a season, like Paul, become blind in the very act of conversion. And this he would do without so much as one allusion to himself, without a word of reflection upon others, save when any given art fell naturally in the way of his discourse; without one anecdote that was not proof and illustration of a previous position; gratifying no passion, indulging no caprice, but with a calm mastery over your soul, leading you onward and onward forever through a thousand windings, yet with no pause, to some magnificent point in which, as in a focus,

---

**From Carlyle's Life of John Sterling.* 1851.

Appendix

all the parti-coloured rays of his discourse should converge in light. In all these he was, in truth, your teacher and guide; but in a little while you might forget that he was other than a fellow-student and the companion of your way—so playful was his manner, so simple his language, so affectionate the glance of his eye.*

THE COMPOSITION OF THE ANCIENT MARINER

In the course of this walk was planned the poem of *The Ancient Mariner*, founded on a dream, as Mr. Coleridge said, of his friend Mr. Cruikshank. Much the greatest part of the story was Mr. Coleridge's invention, but certain parts I suggested: for example, some crime was to be committed which should bring upon the Old Navigator, as Coleridge afterwards delighted to call him, the spectral persecution, as a consequence of that crime and his own wanderings. I had been reading in Shelvocke's *Voyages*, a day or two before, that, while doubling Cape Horn, they frequently saw albatrosses in that latitude, the largest sort of sea-fowl, some extending their wings twelve or thirteen feet. 'Suppose,' said I, 'you represent him as having killed one of these birds on entering the South Sea and that the tutelary spirits of these regions take upon them to avenge the crime.' The incident was thought fit for the purpose and adopted accordingly. I also suggested the navigation of the ship by the dead men, but do not remember that I had anything more to do with the scheme of the poem. . . . We began the composition together on that, to me, memorable evening. I furnished two or three lines at the beginning of the poem, in particular:

        And listened like a three years' child;
        The Mariner had his will.*

FROM SHELVOCKE'S VOYAGE'S

. . . . nor one sea bird, except a disconsolate black albatross, who accompanied us for several days, hovering about us as if he had lost himself, till Hatley (my second captain), observing in one of his melancholy fits that this bird was always hovering near us, imagined from his color that it might be some ill-omen. That which, I suppose, induced him the more to encourage his superstition was the continued series of contrary tempestuous winds which had oppressed us ever since we got up into this sea. But be that as it would, he, after some fruitless

---

*From *Table-Talk*, edited by Henry Nelson Coleridge.
*Dictated by Wordsworth to Miss Fenwick in 1842.

Appendix

attempts, at length shot the albatross, not doubting that we should have a fair wind after it.[7]

WORDSWORTH AND THE ANCIENT MARINER

When . . . Mr. Wordsworth was last in London, soon after the appearance of De Quincey's papers in *Tait's Magazine* in 1834-35, he dined with me . . . and made the following statement, which, I am quite sure, I give to you correctly: *The Ancient Mariner* was founded on a strange dream, which a friend of Coleridge had, who fancied he saw a skeleton ship with figures in it. . . . Beside the lines, . . .

> And thou art long, and lank, and brown,
> As is the ribbed sea-sand,

I wrote the stanza, . . .

> He holds him with his glittering eye—
> The Wedding Guest stood still,
> And listens like a three years' child:
> The Mariner hath his will,

and four or five lines more in different parts of the poem, which I could not now point out.[8]

PLAN OF THE LYRICAL BALLADS

During the first year that Mr. Wordsworth and I were neighbors, our conversation turned frequently on the two cardinal points of poetry, the power of exciting the sympathy of the reader by a faithful adherence to the truth of nature, and the power of giving the interest of novelty by the modifying colors of the imagination. The sudden charm which accidents of light and shade, which moonlight or sunset, diffused over a known and familiar landscape, appeared to represent the practicability of combining both. These are the poetry of nature. The thought suggested itself (to which of us I do not recollect) that a series of poems might be composed of two sorts. In the one, the incidents and agents were to be, in part at least, supernatural; and the excellence aimed at was to consist in the interesting of the affections by the dramatic truth of such emotions as would naturally accompany such situations, supposing them real. . . . In this idea originated the plan of the *Lyrical Ballads;* in which

---

[7] Shelvocke. *Voyage Round the World by the Way of the Great South Sea.* 1726.

[8] Alexander Dyce, in a letter to H. N. Coleridge, published e 1852 edition of Coleridge's works.

Appendix

it was agreed that my endeavors should be directed to persons and characters supernatural or at least romantic; yet so as to transfer from our inward nature a human interest and a semblance of truth sufficient to procure for these shadows of imagination that willing suspension of disbelief for the moment, which constitutes poetic faith. Mr. Wordsworth, on the other hand, was to propose to himself as his object to give the charm of novelty to things of every day, and to excite a feeling analogous to the supernatural, by awakening the mind's attention from the lethargy of custom and directing it to the loveliness and the wonder of the world before us. . . . With this view I wrote *The Ancient Mariner.*[*]

THE PURPOSE OF THE ANCIENT MARINER

Mrs. Barbauld once told me that she admired *The Ancient Mariner* very much, but that there were two faults in it—it was improbable and had no moral. As for the probability, I owned that that might admit some question; but as to the want of a moral, I told her that, in my judgment, the poem had too much, and that the only or chief fault, if I might say so, was the obtrusion of the moral sentiment so openly on the reader as a principle or cause of action in a work of such pure imagination. It ought to have no more moral than the *Arabian Nights'* tale of the merchant's sitting down to eat dates by the side of a well, and throwing the shells aside, and lo! a geni starts up, and says he must kill the aforesaid merchant, because one of the dateshells had, it seemed, put out the eye of the geni's son."

PROJECTED COMPLETION OF CHRISTABEL

The following relation was to have occupied a third and fourth canto, and to have closed the tale. Over the mountains, the Bard, as directed by Sir Leoline, hastes with his disciple; but in consequence of one of those inundations supposed to be common to this country, the spot only where the castle once stood is discovered—the edifice itself being washed away. He determines to return. Geraldine, being acquainted with all that is passing, like the weird sisters in *Macbeth*, vanishes. Reappearing, however, she awaits the return of the Bard, exciting in the meantime, by her wily arts, all the anger she could rouse in the Baron's breast, as well as that jealousy of which he is described to have been susceptible. The old Bard and the youth at length arrive, and therefore she can no longer personate the

*Coleridge, *Biographia Literaria*, chap. xiv. 1817.
"Coleridge, *Table-Talk*. May 31, 1830.

Appendix

character of Geraldine, the daughter of Lord Roland de Vaux, but changes her appearance to that of the accepted though absent lover of Christabel. Now ensues a courtship most distressing to Christabel, who feels, she knows not why, great disgust for her once-favored knight. This coldness is very painful to the Baron, who has no more conception than herself of the supernatural transformation. She at last yields to her father's entreaties, and consents to approach the altar with this hated suitor. The real lover, returning, enters at this moment, and produces the ring which she had once given him in sign of her betrothment. Thus defeated, the supernatural being, Geraldine, disappears. As predicted, the castle bell tolls, the mother's voice is heard, and, to the exceeding great joy of the parties, the rightful marriage takes place, after which follows a reconciliation and explanation between father and daughter."

---

[11] Gillman, *Life of Coleridge*, 1838.